Berlitz®

KT-492-427

Cape Town

Berlitz Publishing Company, Inc.

Princeton   Mexico City   London   Eschborn   Singapore

Copyright © 2000 Berlitz Publishing Company, Inc.
400 Alexander Park, Princeton, NJ, 08540 USA
9-13 Grosvenor St., London, W1X 9FB UK

All rights reserved. No part of this book may be reproduced or transmitted in any form or by any means, electronic or mechanical, including photocopying, recording or by any information storage or retrieval system without permission in writing from the publisher.

Berlitz Trademark Reg. U.S. Patent Office and other countries
Marca Registrada

Text:	Karen Coe and Chris Coe
Editor:	Media Content Marketing, Inc.
Photography:	Chris Coe
Cover Photo:	Chris Coe
Photo Editor:	Naomi Zinn
Layout:	Media Content Marketing, Inc.
Cartography:	Rafaelle Degennaro

Although the publisher tries to insure the accuracy of all the information in this book, changes are inevitable and errors may result. The publisher cannot be responsible for any resulting loss, inconvenience, or injury. If you find an error in this guide, please let the editors know by writing to Berlitz Publishing Company, 400 Alexander Park, Princeton, NJ 08540-6306.

ISBN 2-8315-6983-4

Printed in Italy

020/104 RP

CONTENTS

• A (☞ in the text denotes a highly recommended sight

Cape Town

CAPE TOWN AND ITS PEOPLE

From the first sight of the unmistakable profile of Table Mountain, Cape Town works its way into your heart. It is easy to fall in love with the city, and each year many hundreds of thousands of people from all over the world do just that. Cosmopolitan Cape Town is the leading tourist attraction on the African continent, and two-thirds of all visitors to South Africa include it on their itinerary.

The inimitable blend of African, European, and Islamic influences that gives Cape Town its true magic is evident immediately, and it is mesmerizing. One minute you feel as if you're standing in 18th-century Holland, gazing up at an elegant, gabled building. The next you are in a noisy African craft market, with splashes of brightly-colored fabrics alongside carved masks. Then you turn the corner and stroll through what looks like a Victorian English park, with gray squirrels darting amongst the trees. Further on, the narrow, cobbled streets of the Bo-Kaap echo with the sound of the *muezzins* in the minarets calling the faithful to prayer.

This cultural mix infuses all aspects of Cape Town life. Township jazz rings out from small bars. Galleries exhibit the best of African and European art. A wealth of shops, craft and flea markets sell everything from antiques to African carvings, traditional garments to designer clothes, and gourmet food to fresh fruit and aromatic spices. Fine restaurants offer choices from the best of international cuisine to the distinctive local "Cape Malay" dishes, developed here over centuries. People sit at shady sidewalk cafés sipping South African wine and watching street entertainers; expensive yachts dance on the water, mingling with brightly-painted fishing boats, sleek cruise liners, and huge container ships laden with cargo from around the world.

Superb museums chronicle the region's history, stretching beyond the days of the early settlers, European explorers, and even the nomadic hunter-gatherers that first lived there. The exhibits don't just portray a rose-colored vision of the past. Cape Town's history encompasses brutality and bloodshed, the displacement of the original native peoples, slavery, and of course, apartheid. There are reminders everywhere: slave lodges in the courtyards of fine mansions; dioramas of ancient peoples whose way of life was overturned by the arrival of the European setters; the undeveloped land and poignant museum in District Six (see page 33), a graphic testimony to the divisiveness of apartheid. Finally, there is Robben Island, now a museum, but more importantly, a symbol of hope. The world remembers it as the prison that held Nelson Mandela for so many years, yet its legacy of almost unbelievable cruelty extends back for more than 300 years. No punches are pulled here; the simple, dignified presentation of the facts is all that's needed to leave visitors reeling.

Towering above all this activity, rising up like a benevolent giant, is Table Mountain. It first beckoned European seafarers here over five hundred years ago, and continues to enthrall visitors. Wherever you are in the city, it is impossible not to lift your eyes to catch yet another glimpse. Over half a million people travel to the summit each year, to be greeted by magnificent views of the city, the mountains, and the ocean, and walk amongst the fascinating wildlife and flora to be found at the top of this legendary landmark.

Perhaps the greatest pleasure gained from visiting Cape Town comes from its inhabitants. The people are charming and friendly, and everywhere you go you're greeted with a smile. Desmond Tutu famously called South Africa "the

Rainbow Nation," and this best sums up the ethnic mix that is Cape Town. The main racial groups are African, "*Coloured*," Muslim, and white. The African population is descended from those who moved into South Africa from the center of the African continent centuries ago. The Coloured population evolved through the intermingling of the earliest inhabitants: the San bushmen, Khoikhoi herders, descendants of the slaves from the East Indies, members of African tribes from the north and east, and European settlers. Other descendants of the slaves retained their Islamic faith, and are today known as the Cape Muslims. The white population, including the Afrikaners, is mainly of Dutch, British, French, or German origin. The distinct Afrikaner identity evolved in the early 19th century.

Slip out of the summer sun and enjoy a fresh fruit juice at a quayside café in Cape Town.

Company's Gardens offer a bit of relaxation during a long day of sightseeing.

Cape Town is blessed with a Mediterranean climate, and there's never really a "bad" time to go there. Though summer (September–March) sees long days of bright sunshine and temperatures approaching 30°C (86°F), there is much to be said for visiting at other times of the year, not least that you avoid the crowds. Perhaps the city's best-kept secret is that the Cape is at its most beautiful between April and October. Yes, there is rain, but mostly at night, and the temperatures are still mild. The tourist board has recently launched an initiative to promote the "Secret Season," the winter/spring period when the region's flowers are at their spectacular best, and whales migrate along the coast.

As if the wealth of attractions in this vibrant city aren't enough, within a short distance lies an incredible richness of natural beauty. There are mountains everywhere: towering over verdant winelands, cradling picturesque Victorian towns, flanking dense, hardwood forests, and stretching down towards colorful fishing villages or vast expanses of white-sand beaches to sparkling waters teeming with marine life.

Much of this can be explored on day-long excursions from the city. You can follow one of the Wine Routes, through towns such as Stellenbosch and Franschhoek, sampling some of the best South African wines while sitting in a vineyard, enjoying spectacular mountain views. Or walk for miles along empty stretches of pristine white sand, spotting whales and dolphins out at sea and decades-old shipwrecks on the beach, then eat delicious seafood in an open-air restaurant set on the shore. Follow in the footsteps of the elephants who once roamed through the lush hardwood forests of the Tsitsikamma Mountains (along the Garden Route), or spend a day marveling at the astounding variety of colorful plants, trees, and flowers in the Kirstenbosch National Botanical Gardens.

More than any country in the world, South Africa has been notorious for its history of racial prejudice and segregation, and the haunting legacy of those days can still be seen in the Cape Flats, the desolate black townships where poverty and crime still prevail. However, heartfelt efforts by all sides to come together are slowly working. You'll still find people who claim that life was better under apartheid, but they are few and far between. The average white Capetonian is appalled by what happened, and eager to heal the wounds. There is still a great divide between rich and poor, but this is increasingly less along racial lines. Righting the wrongs of the past is a massive undertaking, but the will to succeed is strong.

The city has earned an unenviable reputation as a place where crime is rife. The fact that there are problems is undeniable, but no more than in any other major city. A few basic precautions are all that's needed to have a trouble-free visit. Don't be alarmed by ominous stories of crime, or you'll spend your visit looking over your shoulder, and miss one of the most captivating cities in the world.

With so much to do and see, it's easy to see why travelers decide to go to Cape Town; and once you are there, you'll find it hard to go home. Chances are, when you leave, you'll be planning what to do on your next visit.

A BRIEF HISTORY

Cape Town has earned many nicknames over the years, but perhaps the most apt is the "Mother City." Since the arrival of the first Europeans, it has been the center for the foundation of modern South Africa.

For tens of thousands of years, this region was the domain of the San bushmen, nomadic hunter-gathers living off the wealth of game. Beautiful San rock paintings can be seen around the Western Cape, especially in the Cederberg Wilderness Area. The South African Museum in the city center has some excellent examples preserved in display cases.

Some two thousand years ago, Khoikhoi cattle herders moved into the area. Although this displaced the San, forcing them inland, the two peoples enjoyed an essentially peaceful co-existence, punctuated by occasional skirmishes. The Khoikhoi tended their herds and traded in cattle with the Bantu-speaking people of the north, and the San continued to hunt game.

The Explorers Arrive

This idyllic life was to change forever in the course of less than 200 years. In the late 15th century, the great European powers were engaged in a race to find the best sea route to India, with tremendous wealth from trade in spices and slaves awaiting those who were successful.

In 1488, in his quest to discover the spice route, Portuguese navigator Bartolomeu Dias became the first European to set foot in South Africa. Drawn by the spectacle of Table Mountain, visible from over 150 km (over 90 miles) out at sea, he rounded the Cape and anchored in an inlet in search of fresh water and provisions. He named this area Aguado de Sao Bras (Watering Place of St. Blaize). Today

The San bushmen are not to be forgotten — their rock paintings tell many tales of their history.

this is Mossel Bay, the start of the famous Garden Route. It houses a marvelous museum commemorating Dias (see page 68), with exhibits including a painstakingly reproduced replica of Dias's original ship.

Dias never found the route to India, but he entered the history books as the first person to sail around what became named *Cabo de Boa Esperanza* (the Cape of Good Hope).

Ten years later a second Portuguese navigator, Vasco da Gama, sailed around the Cape and went on to reach India, founding the Spice Route.

The Cape of Good Hope became a vital stopping-off point for ships traveling to the Indies from Europe, with the Khoikhoi soon establishing a thriving trading relationship with the crews. To keep in touch with home during the lengthy voyages, letters were left by sailors under "post office stones," to be collected by homeward-bound vessels. Examples of these stones can be seen in the South African Cultural History Museum in Cape Town (see page 26).

The land adjacent to Table Bay was first explored by Europeans in 1503, when yet another Portuguese explorer, Antonio de Saldanha, climbed the great, flat-topped mountain. He named it Table Mountain, carving a cross into the rock at Lion's Head which can still be seen.

The link with Europe was to remain largely unobtrusive for almost two centuries. Ships would call in, stock up, and move on. The Cape was renowned for its great beauty — in 1580 Sir Francis Drake wrote that it was "the fairest Cape in the whole circumference of the earth" — but also for the ferocity of the storms which raged off its shores. A vivid reminder of these dangerous times can be found in the ship-

Bartolomeu Dias may have been the first European to arrive in South Africa, but certainly not the last.

wreck exhibits in the Victoria Ship Museum at Cape Town's Victoria and Alfred Waterfront (see page 37).

Colonization Begins

In 1652, the Cape of Good Hope fell under the gaze of the mighty Dutch East India Company. Formed by the amalgamation of a number of small trading companies in the early 17th century, the Company had grown in just 50 years to be one of the most powerful organizations on earth, with its own army and fleet. Table Bay was considered an ideal location for one of the Company's bases, to grow food for the crews of its ships and serve as a repair station and hospital. Jan Van Riebeeck, a 23-year-old surgeon, was charged with setting up the post.

Van Riebeeck built a small mud fort on the site where the Castle of Good Hope now stands, and established the Company's Gardens to grow fresh fruit and vegetables. (Known as the Gardens, this is now a popular park in the heart of the city center.) After plans to work the land with local Khoikhoi labor foundered, slaves were imported from the East Indies. In 1666, the foundations were laid for a much larger fort, and the pentagonal Castle of Good Hope was built. These early years are chronicled in the Military Museum at the Castle (see page 23).

The settlement spread into the surrounding countryside, as grain farming began near what is now the suburb of Rondebosch, and, to further expand, some of the Dutch East India Company's servants were allowed to become independent farmers. The land which had for so long been the sole domain of the San and the Khoikhoi became the property of the Dutch, with Van Riebeeck laying claim to an area near what is now Wynberg, where in 1658 he planted the first large-scale vineyard in South Africa.

The Khoikhoi attempted to expel the Europeans in 1659, but they failed. With the subsequent influx of French and German immigrants in the early 18th century displacing them further, Khoikhoi society began to fall apart, and was decimated by a smallpox epidemic in 1713. The nomadic San moved further afield, but were often attacked by settlers. Some were even shot and stuffed by trophy hunters. Many San and Khoikhoi eventually intermingled, their descendants becoming part of what is known today as the *Coloured* population.

Governor Simon Van der Stel was an important influence on the Cape in the latter part of the 17th century. He founded the South African wine industry, building some of the most beautiful mansions and great estates on the Western Cape. Many fine examples of these supremely elegant Cape Dutch buildings still remain.

From 1680 onward, religious refugees began to arrive from Europe, including Huguenots from France, who planted vineyards around what became known as Franschhoek.

By 1750 the original tiny settlement founded by Jan Van Riebeeck was a small town named Kaapstad — Cape Town — that had over 2,500 inhabitants. A second port opened at Simon's Bay (today's Simon's Town), providing a far safer refuge than the turbulent Table Bay, where shipwrecks were all-too-common and countless lives were lost to the sea.

British Influence

In 1795, Britain seized control of Cape Town, and thus the sea route to the East, at the Battle of Muizenberg. Under British rule, the monopolies imposed by the Dutch East India Company to protect its own interests were abolished, and much freer trade began. Cape Town became a sea port of international importance, and the town's cosmopolitan character was firmly established.

The picturesque gateway of the Houses of Parliament — the scene of several dramatic events in South African history.

The Cape again became the property of the Dutch in 1803, but the British regained control at the Battle of Blaauwberg, and it formally became a British colony in 1814. Major companies established offices here, and within a few short years much of the infrastructure that supported the historic city center was in place. In 1815, the first postal packet service began, with ships sailing between Cape Town and England. This eventually led to the first passenger cruise liners, and was the start of the long-standing association between the city and the Union-Castle shipping line, whose 19th-century headquarters building can be seen at the V&A Waterfront (see page 37).

The small settlements around Cape Town started to grow. Simon's Bay became home to the navy, was renamed Simon's Town, and developed a thriving fishing and whaling industry. Under the influence of talented architects such as Louis Michel

Thibault and the sculptor Anton Anreith — both of whom arrived in the Cape as soldiers — houses and commercial buildings of enduring beauty were built. Anreith's fine work is evident throughout the region, with important examples including the magnificent Kat Balcony of the Castle of Good Hope (see page 23), and the pulpit of the Groote Kerk (see page 26).

In 1834 slavery was abolished by the British, and religious freedom was granted. This wasn't an entirely altruistic move; it cost more to keep slaves than to pay wages. The primarily Muslim ex-slaves soon established their own close community in Cape Town's Bo-Kaap.

The City Evolves

In the 1860s, work started on the building of the Victoria and Alfred docks to meet the pressing need for a safe harbor to accommodate the numerous cargo ships now making port at Cape Town.

By the end of the 19th century, the little village of Cape Town had changed beyond recognition. The discovery of gold and diamonds in the east of South Africa led to the building of railways linking what was now a substantial city to other rapidly-developing areas of Africa, and the streets were lined with magnificent banks

The stately façade of City Hall — the site of Nelson Mandela's historic speech.

and commercial buildings, fine mansions, and large department stores. The prime minister of the Cape, Cecil John Rhodes, built a splendid estate at Rondebosch, and bequeathed a vast plot of land at the foot of Table Mountain to the nation. Here the world-famous Kirstenbosch National Botanical Gardens were established, now one of the main tourist attractions in South Africa.

In 1910, eight years after the end of the bloody Boer Wars, the opposing sides — the British and the Dutch-speaking Boers of the Eastern Cape — came together to form the Union of South Africa. Cape Town became the legislative capital of the newly unified country, a role it fulfills to this day.

The Apartheid Era

Although African cooperation had helped the British to victory, Africans didn't benefit from the unification of South Africa. The new government began to issue decrees from the Houses of Parliament in Cape Town that eroded the rights of non-whites. From 1913, their right to own property was severely restricted, and from 1936 they were unable to vote.

When the National Party came to power in 1948 under D. F. Malan, it pledged to introduce influx control, to stop what was felt to be excessive numbers of black workers moving to major cities. It would eventually bring in nationwide, compulsory, racial segregation, initiating the abhorrent apartheid regime.

By the 1960s, African workers were concentrated in the grim shantytowns and men-only hostels of the Cape Flats, forbidden to bring their families to live with them. A peaceful demonstration in Cape Town by inhabitants of the Langa township in 1960 resulted in the deaths of three protestors that were shot by police, fueling the armed struggle against this oppression. High-profile opponents of apartheid, including Nelson Mandela and Walter Sisulu, were sentenced to lengthy incarcerations on Robben Island, a bleak prison located off the coast of Cape Town.

The Group Areas Act of 1966 further oppressed the African and Coloured communities, forcibly evicting them from their homes and moving them out of the city to the Cape Flats. The stirring exhibits at the District Six Museum are an emotional testimony to the despair felt by the inhabitants of these areas. Finally, in 1972, Coloured representation on the town council was abolished.

A New Start

In the 1980s, Cape Town, like all of South Africa, underwent tremendous change as the fight against apartheid took hold. The strongest-yet anti-apartheid force, the United Democratic Front, was formed on the Cape Flats in 1983. In protest against the violent oppression suffered by the non-whites, many countries imposed harsh economic sanctions on South Africa. These proved crippling, hugely damaging Cape Town by depriving it of the cargo ships that were its lifeblood. South Africans were banned from international sporting events — a particularly wounding blow to such a sports-loving country.

In 1986 history was made at St. George's Cathedral, Cape Town, when Desmond Tutu was enthroned as South Africa's first black archbishop.

In 1990 the city became the focus of the eyes of the world, when in a surprise initiative by President F.W. de Klerk, Nelson Mandela was released after 27 years in prison. Within hours of his release, Mandela stood on the balcony of Cape Town's City Hall, addressing a crowd of over 100,000 people standing on Grand Parade below him. This historical moment was witnessed by millions of people on televisions all over the world.

Four years later, Nelson Mandela became the first black president of South Africa, and from the Parliament in Cape

Town, began the delicate process of peaceful reconciliation after centuries of racial conflict.

Today the "Mother City" continues to play a crucial role in the welfare of her country, with all laws emanating from the city's Houses of Parliament.

Cape Town is also the scene of international sporting events. Although the recent bid for the 2004 Olympics was unsuccessful, it further raised the profile of this very special place, and plans are underway to bid for the 2008 event. Cape Town is also a major contender to host the 2006 soccer World Cup.

Marvel at the bird's-eye view of sprawling Cape Town from atop Table Mountain.

The tiny settlement Jan van Riebeeck established in 1652 is now one of the most important centers of commerce on the African continent. It is home to the South African headquarters of numerous major international corporations, and foreign investment is growing all the time. The cosmopolitan sophistication, outstanding location, and relaxed atmosphere of Cape Town also acts as a magnet to those involved in the creative industries. Advertising agencies, filmmakers, designers, and architects abound, and many renowned artists have chosen to make their home in and around this beautiful city.

Cape Town, and its people, are moving forward with hope, enthusiasm, and energy.

Historical Landmarks

1488 Bartolomeu Dias rounds the Cape of Good Hope.

1498 Vasco da Gama discovers the Spice Route to India.

1503 Antonio de Saldanha names Table Mountain.

1652 Jan Van Riebeeck establishes a Dutch East India Company post at Table Bay.

1658 Slaves first imported to the Cape, and first large-scale vineyard planted.

1666 Foundations laid for the Castle of Good Hope.

1679 Simon Van der Stel becomes Governor of the Cape.

1680 German and French settlers arrive.

1795 The British take control of Cape Town with the Battle of Muizenberg.

1803 Cape Town given back to the Dutch under the Treaty of Amiens.

1806 The British re-take the Cape in the Battle of Blaauwberg.

1814 Congress of Vienna cedes the Cape to the British.

1834 Slavery abolished.

1860 The docks and harbor are built.

1880 By this year, railways link Cape Town to much of the African subcontinent.

1910 The Union of South Africa is established. Cape Town becomes the seat of the country's legislature.

1948 The National Party comes to power, subsequently introducing apartheid.

1960 Police kill anti-apartheid protestors during a demonstration.

1963 Nelson Mandela is imprisoned on Robben Island.

1966 Group Areas Act relocates African and Coloured communities to the Cape Flats.

1983 United Democratic Front is formed on the Cape Flats.

1986 Desmond Tutu becomes first black archbishop.

1990 Mandela released and makes his landmark speech from the balcony of Cape Town City Hall.

1994 Mandela becomes President of South Africa.

WHERE TO GO

CITY CENTER

Cape Town is a joy to explore. Part of its charm lies in its small size. You can see most of the historic highlights in just a few hours' easy walking, while a relatively undemanding day's exploring will really give you a sense of knowing the place. Be aware, though, that the African sun can get very hot, so take your time, wear a hat, and drink lots of water.

Like many American cities, Cape Town is laid out on a grid system, and it is easy to find your way around. Numerous tours and historic walks are available, but you can easily make your own itinerary.

Historic City Center

The **Castle of Good Hope,** on Castle Street, is the oldest European building in South Africa. This pentagonal fort, which has recently undergone extensive restoration, replaced the original wooden fortress established by Jan Van Riebeeck as the headquarters of the Dutch East India Company. It took 13 years to construct, and was finished in 1679. For 150 years the Castle was the heart of administrative, social, and eco-

The Castle of Good Hope is the oldest European building in South Africa.

Enjoy the lush blooms and soft bouquets in the Trafalgar Place Flower Market.

nomic life on the Cape. Today it still retains an active military purpose, as the headquarters for the Western Province Command of the Defence Force, and Changing of the Guard takes place daily, at noon. Viewed from the outside, the Castle is unimpressive and has few claims to beauty, but its merit lies in its historical interest.

Three museum collections are housed here. The Military Museum relates the story of the early years of Dutch East India Company's presence on the Cape; the rooms of the Secunde's House, originally the home of the deputy governor, are furnished in the style of the 16th and 17th centuries, while the marvelous William Fehr Collection of paintings, furniture, china, and porcelain in the Governor's Residence is well worth a visit. This last building is adorned by the Kat Balcony, with its magnificent sculpture by Anton Anreith. Free official tours are given around the ramparts, dungeon, torture chamber, and armories, and there is a good restaurant/tea shop in the courtyard.

Opposite the Castle, across Buitenkant Street, lies **Grand Parade,** where vast crowds gathered to hear Nelson Mandela's first speech upon being released from prison. A lively flea market operates here every Wednesday and Saturday. South of the Castle lies District Six (see pages 33 and 80).

City Hall, with the balcony where Mandela made that historic speech, is on Darling Street. Built in the Italian Renaissance style in 1905, it is home to the City Library and Cape Town Symphony Orchestra. Entrance is free to view this splendid example of Edwardian opulence, with its ornate stained-glass window commemorating England's King Edward VII and Queen Alexandra.

If you walk up Darling Street you come to **Adderley Street,** named in honor of Charles Adderley, a 19th-century British politician. He earned the gratitude of the residents of Cape Town when he helped them to resist attempts by the British government to establish a penal colony at the Cape. Once a prestigious residential area for prominent local families, Adderley Street is now a major commercial thoroughfare.

To your right, don't miss the vivid, gloriously-scented blooms in the **Trafalgar Place Flower Market** — enjoy the lively banter of the Bo-Kaap women as you browse. The ugly, concrete 1970s facade of Golden Acre Mall does nothing for the appearance of this area, but it is full of excellent shops.

On the corner of Adderley and Darling Streets stands the rather splendid **Standard Bank,** distinguished by its tall dome atop which sits a statue of Britannia. Cecil Rhodes

Take a tour or catch a live parliamentary session in the Houses of Parliament.

used to bank here. This is the first of a series of important historical buildings lining Adderley Street. Another example of fine commercial architecture can be found at the **First National Bank,** which has retained its huge circular wooden writing desk complete with original inkwells.

A little further along, on your left-hand side, you'll find the Mother Church of the Dutch Reformed Faith, the **Groote Kerk** (entrance on Church Square). Here, the important Afrikaans families of Cape Town worshiped in the second half of the 19th century, and one can view the enclosed pews. Each has its own door, so social distinctions could be maintained, even at prayer. A church has existed here since 1678, but the present building was erected in 1841. The enormous carved pulpit by sculptor Anton Anreith and carpenter Jan Graaff was originally installed in the previous church on this site. Crafted from Burmese teak,

with lion-shaped supports made from stinkwood, it is truly outstanding.

At the top of Adderley Street is the quaint **South African Cultural History Museum.** This was originally the Slave Lodge for those who worked in the Company's Gardens. It later became a brothel, and in 1810 served a somewhat different purpose, as government offices, housing the Supreme Court.

The proud figure of Cecil Rhodes still presides over Company's Gardens.

Displays include weapons, furniture, toys and ceramics from the days of the early settlers, plus African tribal art. The exhibit on the history of the city is particularly interesting.

From Adderley Street, continue along tree-lined Government Avenue, a pedestrian walkway forming the heart of the historic center of Cape Town. On the left, with the main entrance on Parliament Street, lie the **Houses of Parliament,** scene of so many dramatic events in the turbulent history of South Africa. Tickets to watch parliamentary sessions or tour the buildings are available (see page 79).

> The only taxis which can be hailed from the street are the three-wheeled Rikkis. The others are available from taxi ranks or can be ordered by phone.

De Tuynhuis, the official office of the President of South Africa, is next to the Houses of Parliament. Originally the Guest House for the Dutch East India Company, it was remodeled extensively by a succession of governors to become the fine building you see today.

In 1652, Jan Van Riebeeck established South Africa's first market garden to supply fresh fruit and vegetables to the merchant ships of the Dutch East India Company. The 3 hectares (7 acres) of elegant parkland you see in the **Company's Gardens** is all that remains of the original 17 hectares (43 acres). At the end of the 17th century, rather than continue to grow its own produce, the Company granted land to independent farmers and bought food from them.

The Gardens were transformed into a botanic garden for the Cape Town elite. It is a delightful place with exotic plants, fountains, shady paths, and rose gardens. Near the outdoor café stands an ancient saffron pear tree, reputed to have been brought from Holland in the 17th century. A statue of Cecil Rhodes presides over the central path, and an army of gray

*Discover the four-story-high Whale Well in the South
African Museum — the county's largest and oldest museum.*

squirrels busily darts around, the descendants of those
Rhodes introduced to South Africa over 100 years ago.

Next to the Gardens is the **South African Library.** One of
the first free libraries in the world, it houses an immense collection of rare books.

Beyond Rhodes' statue you come to the country's
largest and oldest museum, the **South African Museum.**
A magnificent building with Table Mountain as its back-
drop; this is a truly wonderful place, with plenty to interest both young and old. It is primarily dedicated to natural history. Notable exhibits include dioramas of prehistoric
life and a four-story-high Whale Well. The latter contains
the huge skeleton of a blue whale. The anthropological
exhibits are not to be missed either, including remarkable
depictions of 19th-century San tribal life, and some truly
superb rock art.

The **Planetarium** adjoining the Museum has daily shows, some specifically for children, providing an excellent opportunity to learn more about the night sky of the southern hemisphere.

Across Government Avenue from the South African Museum you will find the eclectic **South African National Gallery.** This originally displayed mainly European art, and still contains a number of works by renowned artists such as Gainsborough and Reynolds. However, the primary focus is now on contemporary South African art, and there is a growing collection of traditional tribal work, including carvings and beadwork.

The nearby **Jewish Museum** on Hatfield Street is housed in the oldest synagogue in the country. The history of Jewish life in South Africa is chronicled through photographs, art, and books in this opulent building.

On Orange Street at the far end of Government Avenue is a Cape Town landmark: the sugar-pink **Mount Nelson Hotel,** the most luxurious hotel in the city. "The Nellie" has been an integral part of city life since 1899. During the Boer War, a young journalist by the name of Winston Churchill was often to be seen pacing its corridors. Afternoon tea in its magnificent landscaped gardens is a memorable civilized occasion.

Facing back up Government Avenue from the Mount Nelson Hotel, turn left along Orange Street to **Long Street,** a fascinating mix of bygone elegance and more recent sleaziness combined with architectural diversity. Elaborate Georgian and Victorian houses with ornate wrought-iron balconies echo the architecture of New Orleans, and minarets mark the mosques that draw the Muslims of the nearby Bo-Kaap. Long Street was once notorious for its drinking dens and brothels, and to some extent these still survive, alongside shops selling everything from second-hand books to antique furniture and period clothing. A visit to the steam rooms of the **Long Street Baths** is a great way to unwind after a day's sightseeing.

The **Sendinggestig Museum** is an oasis of calm on Long Street. The first church for Africans, this pretty peach-and-white building now contains exhibits portraying the history of mission work in South Africa.

Across Long Street, just around the corner from Strand Street, is the **Koopmans de Wet House.** This elegant structure, with its delicate, Neo-Classical pink-and-white façade, sits like a doll's house between towering office blocks. Built in 1701, it enjoyed the height of its fame as home to socialite and art collector, Maria Koopmans de Wet (1834–1906). Extravagantly decorated rooms furnished in late 18th-century European style stand in stark contrast to the slave quarters.

Further along Strand Street is South Africa's first **Lutheran Church.** German immigrants had to worship in the Dutch Reformed Church until 1771, and merchant Martin Melck celebrated their religious emancipation by funding the building of this splendid church. Anton Anreith carved the wooden pulpit, which was so admired that he was asked to make one for the Groote Kerk on Adderley Street. Next to the Lutheran Church is Martin Melck House, the former parsonage, which now contains a restaurant and art gallery.

Turning right, you come to **St. George's Mall,** a busy promenade lined with many shops, stalls and cafés, where

With local crafts stalls, cafés, shops, and more, who can refuse St. George's Mall?

street entertainers perform for the crowds.

St. George's Cathedral, on nearby Wale Street, was the religious seat of Desmond Tutu. From here, in 1989, he led 30,000 people to City Hall where he famously declared to the world, "We are the rainbow people!" The Cathedral owes its Gothic appearance to architect Sir Herbert Baker, who revamped the original 1834 building. Viewed from inside, the stained-glass windows are particularly impressive.

Home of Cape Town's Muslim community, Bo Kaap keeps its rich cultural heritage alive.

If you go down Shortmarket Street and you'll come to cobbled **Greenmarket Square.** The scene of many public announcements, including that of the abolition of slavery in 1834, it is now a colorful, busy souvenir market, where you can bargain for African masks, carvings, fabrics, and jewelry.

The **Old Town House** on Greenmarket Square was built in 1755 as the headquarters of the Burgher Watch, effectively an early combined police force and fire department. This beautiful example of Cape Dutch architecture, once the most important civic building in Cape Town, is now an art gallery, home to the Michaelis Collection of 17th-century Dutch landscape paintings.

Bo-Kaap

Walking along Shortmarket Street out of the other side of Greenmarket Square and across Buitengracht Street brings you to the slopes of Signal Hill, and the **Bo-Kaap,** the home of Cape Town's Muslim community. It is a fascinating place, with 18th- and early 19th-century "cube" houses painted in colorful shades, narrow streets, spice shops, and the minarets of 11 mosques, including South Africa's first official mosque, the Auwal (on Dorp Street).

The inhabitants of the Bo-Kaap are mostly descended from highly-skilled and educated slaves imported into the Cape from the East Indies. They brought with them their faith, Sufism (part of the Islamic religion), and a strong culture which has survived centuries of repression when their language, history, and writing could only be preserved in secret. Although the Cape Muslims are still sometimes erroneously referred to as the "Cape Malays," few of their ancestors actually came from Malaysia. Traders at that time used the Malayal language as a common tongue, hence the name Cape Malays.

> When driving, watch out for oncoming drivers pulling out to overtake. They will assume that you will pull over to the hard shoulder to avoid an accident.

Until 1834 this area was inhabited by Dutch and English artisans, but when slavery was abolished, the freed Muslims moved in. They established a community which was to survive even the notorious Group Areas Act of 1966. Under this, virtually every non-white neighborhood in Cape Town was designated a White Group Area, and razed to the ground to make way for whites-only housing. The original inhabitants moved out of the city.

The **Bo-Kaap Museum** on Wale Street is based around the fine house and possessions of a wealthy 19th-century Muslim family, with exhibits depicting the history of the community.

It is best not to walk alone through this intriguing neighborhood. Join one of the many walking tours that operate here and will include a visit to the Museum.

Standing on the edge of the world! Enjoy the city's majestic landscape from atop a viewing platform on Table Mountain.

District Six Museum

On the other side of the historic city center is a poignant reminder of a Coloured area that couldn't withstand the Group Areas Act. **District Six,** south of the Castle of Good Hope, was once a cosmopolitan neighborhood, with some 60,000 predominantly Coloured inhabitants forming a lively community. In 1966 it was designated a White Group Area, and all non-whites were evicted and moved to the townships.

Over the next 15 years, the buildings of District Six were systematically reduced to rubble. Most of the luxury houses due to take their place were never built, so strong was the national and international outrage at the demolition of the original community. Today the land remains largely undeveloped, and the story of the uprooted residents is told in the intensely moving **District Six Museum,** based in Buitenkant Methodist Church.

Highlights and Must-See Attractions

Bo-Kaap. Intriguing home of Cape Town's Muslim community.

Castle of Good Hope. Oldest European building in South Africa, and the center of Cape life for 150 years.

City Hall. Scene of Nelson Mandela's legendary speech upon release from jail.

Company's Gardens. Wander through this elegant park and remember that the city began with a fruit and vegetable garden on this very site.

Groot Constantia. The first truly great Cape estate and productive vineyard.

Houses of Parliament. The heart of South African legislature.

Kirstenbosch National Botanical Gardens. Glorious collections of indigenous flora in an unrivalled setting on the slopes of Table Mountain. Not to be missed.

Long Street. Architectural diversity and fascinating small shops, all imbued with an air of faded decadence.

Robben Island. For centuries the brutal place of incarceration for political dissidents, this is now an intensely moving museum.

South African Museum. Wonderful rock art, and stunning natural history exhibits.

St George's Cathedral. Where Desmond Tutu declared, "We are the rainbow people!"

Table Mountain. World-famous South African icon. Ride the Cableway (or walk) to the top for breathtaking views of the Western Cape.

Victoria & Alfred Waterfront. Remarkable revitalization of a redundant area, now a key tourist attraction. Restaurants and shops vie for attention with an excellent maritime museum and the superb Two Oceans Aquarium.

Photographs, original street signs, and written recollections of past inhabitants bear vivid witness to the devastating impact of apartheid.

TABLE MOUNTAIN

Standing 1,086 m (over 3,500 ft) tall and measuring nearly 3 km (nearly 2 miles) across, **Table Mountain** was declared a National Monument in 1957. Now a World Heritage Site, it is South Africa's number one tourist attraction. No visit to Cape Town is complete without taking in the unforgettable bird's

> The Muslim community is teetotal, so restaurants specializing in Cape Malay food may not necessarily serve alcohol.

eye views from the summit. All facets of Cape Town life are spread out below in miniature — a myriad of ships in the bay, fine houses in wealthy suburbs, beautiful beaches, historic buildings, soaring skyscrapers, and the grim shantytowns.

The weather at the top of the mountain can change very quickly. One moment it is in sparkling sunshine, the next, shrouded in cloud — the "Tablecloth" that sits on top and spills down over the edges. If you want to go up the mountain, the golden rule is that if you can see the top, go now!

The exhilarating six-minute cable car ride to the top of Table Mountain is, in itself, an adventure to be treasured. The original **Cableway** was opened in 1929 and proved immediately popular. Over 600,000 visitors a year choose to travel to the summit in this way, and to meet this demand, the very latest technology was imported from Switzerland in 1997. The new cable cars revolve 360° in the course of the journey, ensuring that all passengers enjoy every part of the panorama. Letters bearing the Table Mountain postmark can be sent from the souvenir shop at the summit, and there are plenty of viewing platforms and a self-service restaurant.

The indigenous flora and fauna to be found here are truly memorable. Table Mountain is home to almost 1,500 species of plants, some found nowhere else in the world, and the renowned Kirstenbosch National Botanical Gardens run down from its eastern flank. Whatever the season, you're sure to see stunning flowers, such as wild orchids with their glorious range of colors, and other magnificent vegetation including the spectacular Silver Tree. Wildlife is also plentiful, including porcupines, dassies (or "rockrabbits"), grysbok (a small, nocturnal antelope), and baboons.

There are over 300 footpaths on the mountain, ranging from the undemanding to those best tackled only by experts, and it is a sensible precaution to contact Mountain Club of South Africa (Tel. 021/465 3412) or a company such as Walk Up Table Mountain (Tel. 021/415 2503) if you're planning a lengthy hike. In the early morning the mountain slopes are in shade, making climbing a much cooler experience.

The Cableway operates every day, weather permitting, with regular departures from Lower Cable Station. In peak season, book tickets in advance from Lower Cable Station or the V&A Waterfront Visitors Center to avoid a lengthy line.

Table Mountain is flanked by smaller mountains. To the right, when viewed from the city, are **Lion's Head** and **Signal Hill,** and to the left, **Devil's Peak.** The west face of Table Mountain comprises a series of distinctive rock formations called the **Twelve Apostles.** On a clear day you can see the entire city, V&A Waterfront, and Table Bay to the north, Camps Bay and the Twelve Apostles to the west, the mountains of Stellenbosch and the Cape Flats townships in the east, and sometimes even Cape Point to the south, all from within 100 m (325 ft) of the cable car station. A walk along the plateau gives views of the Southern Suburbs down to False Bay in the south.

The views of the city and Table Mountain from Signal Hill Road, which links Lion's Head to Signal Hill, are also outstanding. Signal Hill was originally a signaling post for communication with ships out at sea, and the Noon Gun is still fired from here each day. For a romantic view of the lights of Cape Town set against a floodlit Table Mountain, drive up Signal Hill at night.

VICTORIA AND ALFRED WATERFRONT

The **Victoria and Alfred Waterfront** (V&A) is one of Cape Town's most popular and vibrant attractions. The city's original Victorian harbor was almost derelict for two decades after the cargo ships it was built to accommodate gave way to the supertankers that now dock at nearby Duncan Dock. Redevelopment

Partake in one of the V&A Waterfront's popular attractions, including guided boat tours, museums, and exhibits.

Smile! Check out Two Oceans Aquarium's latest exhibition, aptly entitled "Fangs."

of the area started in the early 1990s. This is now nearing completion, and has succeeded beyond all expectations.

The V&A Waterfront's historic warehouses and dock buildings have been beautifully restored and contain some of the best shops, nightlife, and restaurants in the city. There are also fascinating museums and exhibits, an aquarium, outdoor entertainment, craft markets, a cinema complex, and even a microbrewery. From here you can catch the ferry to Robben Island, and take helicopter and boat trips around the harbor and along the coastline.

The V&A Waterfront comprises three basins — Victoria Basin, Alfred Basin, and New Basin. Alfred Basin is named after Queen Victoria's second son, Prince Alfred, who in 1860 ceremonially tipped the first rock to begin construction of the original harbor. A series of display boards around the site documents its history, and the Visitors Center sells an excellent booklet guiding you on an entertaining historical walk.

The maritime history of the Cape is detailed in full at the **South African National Maritime Museum** on Dock Road. Exhibits include the *S.A.S. Somerset*, the only surviving boom defense vessel in the world (visitors are free to explore the entire ship), and a number of superb models, including a splendid depiction of Cape Town Harbor as it appeared in 1886.

More memories of seafaring life can be found on the **Victoria Museum Ship** at Pierhead. This replica of an 18th-century Frigate houses items salvaged from shipwrecks both on the Cape and around the world. Other attractions reflecting the area's maritime past include the **Time Ball Tower,** once used by navigators in the bay to set their clocks, the **Harbor Master's Residence,** with its glorious, 100-year-old dragon tree, and the pedestrian swing-bridge by the **Old Clock Tower.**

The V&A Waterfront is still an active harbor, and fishing boats, yachts, and cruise liners are all to be seen there. Take to the water yourself on a charter vessel, or ride the **Penny Ferry,** a rowboat service which opened to the public in 1880. The fare for this four-minute journey was originally one penny, and even now it is a very reasonable R2. Look for the Cape fur seals enjoying the waves or sunning themselves on the docks by the Old Clock Tower. A host of other boat tours, and sailing, fishing, and diving excursions can be taken from the V&A Waterfront.

The **Two Oceans Aquarium,** South Africa's largest Aquarium, showcases the unique ecosystem of the Cape Peninsula, with its extraordinary bounty of fish, birds, mammals, reptiles, and plant life from the Indian and Atlantic oceans. Stunning exhibits include a five-story, glass-enclosed kelp forest, and a vast, mesmerizing tank containing sharks, turtles, and numerous other large predators. There are also seal and penguin pools. The newest exhibition, *Fangs*, offers a unique glimpse into the world of sea snakes and eels. Touch pools allow visitors to examine some of the friendlier creatures at first hand. This is a great favorite with children and adults alike. You can also watch the sharks, turtles, and penguins being fed. Qualified scuba divers can swim amongst the ragged-tooth sharks in the Predator Exhibit or dive in the Kelp Forest (booking in advance is essential; Tel. 021/418 3823 or visit the Information Desk at the Aquarium).

With the longest trading hours in the Western Cape, and hundreds of shops, the V&A Waterfront is a shopper's paradise. The main malls are the **Victoria and Alfred Mall** and the **Victoria Wharf Shopping Centre,** while the **V&A Waterfront Craft Market** is the largest in South Africa. You can request a made-to-order item at the **Red Shed Craft Workshop** in Victoria Wharf, then watch it being made.

Children will particularly enjoy the innovative **Telkom Exploratorium** hands-on science exhibit detailing the history of telecommunication, or the chance to find semi-precious gemstones in the Scratch Patch.

An evening at the V&A Waterfront is a must. Lively bars, restaurants, and clubs abound. The **Agfa Amphitheater** has free shows almost every day, ranging from rock and jazz concerts to performances by the Cape Town Symphony Orchestra, while the latest films can be seen at a choice of 18 cinemas. Superb nature documentaries are shown each day on the massive, five-story-high screen at the **IMAX** cinema.

With over a million people passing through its gates each month, the V&A Waterfront bustles day and night. The friendly Visitors Centre on Dock Road (Tel. 021/418 2369) is an excellent source of advice on the latest events and the historic and modern attractions, and arranges bookings for tours and taxis, while the web site <www.waterfront.co.za> provides comprehensive, well-presented information, making it easy to plan your own personal itinerary before you travel. There is ample parking at the Waterfront, and good public transport, including buses and water taxis.

ROBBEN ISLAND

Lying 10 km (6 miles) off the north coast of Cape Town, **Robben Island** is a vivid and poignant reminder of South Africa's troubled political past, for it was here that oppo-

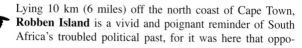

Robben Island, once South Africa's most notorious prisons, now serves as a national museum and wildlife reserve.

nents of apartheid — most famously, Nelson Mandela and Walter Sisulu — were held. An integral part of the country's history, it is now a national museum and wildlife reserve, and an essential itinerary item for visitors to Cape Town.

Mandela spent 19 years in the place he once described as "the harshest, most iron-fisted outpost in the South African penal system," and the tiny cell which was his "home" for nearly two decades has become virtually a shrine for the tens of thousands of tourists who visit each year. Once you have seen it, you can only marvel at this remarkable man, and realize what an incredible moment it was when he returned to that cell during the Millennium celebration to light a candle to mark hope for the future.

Visitors can see the dormitories where dozens of inmates endured appallingly cold and cramped conditions, the lime quarry where prisoners damaged their eyesight working in the unremitting glare, and the house in which Pan-African Congress leader Robert Sobukwe served years of solitary confinement. The leper graveyard and church are a reminder of the other outcasts who shared this man-made hell.

By the time Nelson Mandela arrived on Robben Island in 1963 this tiny island had been infamous for its brutality for over three centuries. It housed political opponents of whatever regime was in power, criminals, the insane, and lepers alike.

Dutch settlers named the island after the "robbe," the seals that lived in the waters off the Cape, and first established a prison there in the mid-1660s. The earliest political prisoner was Autshumato, a Khoikhoi leader banished by the Dutch. A succession of political detainees followed, including Muslim holy men. The mosque close to the prison is a shrine to these men, who were the founders of Islam on the Cape.

From the mid-1800s the island was increasingly used as a hospital. This diversification didn't lessen the brutality. Patients lived in terrible conditions, and the chronically sick afforded no more consideration than criminals or political dissidents.

In spite of its notorious past, Robben Island is seen as a positive symbol. Ahmed Kathrada, head of the Ex-Political Prisoners Committee, who spent almost 20 years there, said, "We want it to reflect the triumph of freedom and human dignity over oppression and humiliation, of courage and determination over weakness, of a new South Africa over the old."

Visiting the island is a moving and remarkable experience. The tour guides, ex-inmates, provide a graphic insight into life, or rather existence, inside the prison. At times it is harrowing and you are left dumbfounded, if not nauseated, by the inhumanity of man to fellow man. Yet the guides communicate with humor and a positive attitude that is both humbling and uplifting. Ex-warders now work alongside those who were once interred here. In A-Wing the prison security intercom system has been ingeniously adapted to relate "Cell Stories." You can activate these to hear the voices of former prisoners describing their experiences.

One aspect of Robben Island that is seldom in the spotlight is its wealth of flora and wildlife. Seventy-four species of bird have been recorded here, including the Cape Jackass penguin and the endangered African Oystercatcher. In the

> **Don't walk alone or take public transport after dark. At night, a metered cab is the safest way to get around the city.**

spring the place is alive with colorful flowers, while the waters around it teem with abalone (a type of large marine snail) and crayfish (rock lobster) year-round.

As the boat leaves at the end of the tour, you may have mixed emotions, but you cannot help feeling a deep admiration for all those that suffered here. That this former purgatory has been transformed into such a remarkable experience is a testimony to the spirit of all who lived under the malignant apartheid regime.

Robben Island is now a World Heritage Site, administered by the Department of Arts, Culture, Science and Technology, which runs the only official tours. Ferries leave each day from the V&A Waterfront. The boats depart every two hours, and tickets are obtained from the Embarkation Office at the Waterfront. Two tours are offered, lasting three or four hours, including the boat trip. To avoid the disappointment of not seeing everything, be sure to take the longer excursion, though even this allows only just enough time. The boats are liable to cancellation out of peak season. Many other operators offer "trips to Robben Island," but be aware that these only include a boat journey around the island; they aren't allowed to land passengers.

Kirstenbosch National Botanical Gardens boasts one of the most important botanical collections in the world.

SOUTHERN SUBURBS

The lush suburbs south of Cape Town are an increasingly popular base from which to explore the city. Extending east from the slopes of Table Mountain and south towards the False Bay coast, they have excellent hotels and guest houses in safe neighborhoods, and great shopping, restaurants, and entertainment. From their comfortable streets, rich in fine Cape Dutch and Victorian houses, it is easy to get to vineyards, forests, and gardens of tremendous beauty, yet they're just 15–20 minutes' drive from the heart of the city.

The fabulous **Kirstenbosch National Botanical Gardens,** south of the suburb of Newlands, form one of the most important botanical collections in the world. They were founded in 1913 by Professor Henry Pearson, on the huge garden site bequeathed to the nation by Cecil Rhodes. Few places on the planet are as rich in floral variety as the Western Cape, and these magnificent gardens contain almost 7,000 species of native wild plants set in an awe-inspiring location under the watchful eye of Table Mountain.

You can easily spend a full day here, following the numerous walking trails. They lead you through densely-planted areas alive with scent and color, up the rocky slopes of Table Mountain to the edge of tree-lined ravines. Other highlights include herb and fragrance gardens and, in all its glorious colors, South Africa's national plant, the protea. There are also specialist collections of cycads — plants which have reputedly remained unchanged since the Jurassic period.

The Gardens are very definitely a must-see item for visitors to Cape Town. Even a few hours spent in their leafy confines will give you an idea of the incredible wealth of flora in this area. There's a restaurant and charming café, and a nursery selling seeds, plants, and books. Sunday evenings during

Carpets of Flowers

Though the smallest of the world's six floral kingdoms, the Cape Floral Kingdom is the richest, boasting an incredible 8,600 species of wild plants, 5,800 of which are found nowhere else on earth.

The most common vegetation is *fynbos* ("fine bushes"). This comprises three families: proteas, which come in all shapes and sizes, all deeply colored; restios, the hardy ground-cover used for thatching; and the delicate ericas, similar to heathers.

The Cape comes alive with spring flowers in September and October, with the most spectacular displays drawing massive crowds. Huge traffic jams build up along routes through vast regions carpeted with brightly colored blooms as far as the eye can see. Many towns and villages hold wildflower festivals at this time of year to celebrate the natural wonder on their doorstep, and Flowerline issues updates (Tel. 021/418 3705).

the summer months, open-air concerts, ranging from jazz to classical to rock are held here. For a lasting memory, bring a picnic and watch the sunset from this beautiful setting.

Many of the paths are hilly and the sun can be very hot, so take your time. There is ample shade, though, and a gentle breeze much of the time. The signage isn't very good, so it is wise to equip yourself with a map before you wander into this botanical heaven. If you have difficulty walking, cart tours are available, and there's a special braille tour for the blind.

On the last Sunday of each month (except June–August), the Kirstenbosch Craft Market is held here. The quality of the goods on sale is strictly controlled by the Botanical Society, who insist that they must be crafted by hand and that the maker of the goods be present at the market. In addition to clothing, ceramics, bead-work, and sculptures, there are also some very good food stalls.

Once the centerpiece of the Simon Van der Stel estate, Groot Constantia still functions as a reminder of its illustrious past.

Constantia is another of the great attractions in the Southern Suburbs. Nestled into the lower slopes of Table Mountain and the Constantiaberg mountains, and enjoying views of False Bay, Constantia was the birthplace of the wine industry in South Africa.

This luscious spot was chosen by the Governor of Cape Town, Simon Van der Stel, for his own estate, out of the vast expanse of rich farmland he was given by the Dutch East India Company. Where the governor led, other high-ranking families followed, and consequently Constantia is rich in beautiful old Cape Dutch architecture. Van der Stel planted the first vines on his estate in 1685.

After Van der Stel's death, his estate was divided into three smaller estates and sold. The largest estate, **Groot Constantia,** is still an active winery, with the added attraction that it contains Van der Stel's original manor house, designed by Louis Thibault. Although badly damaged by fire in 1925, it has been meticulously restored to its original state, and is quite beautiful. The museum in the old cellars features a superb pediment depicting a bacchanalia, sculpted by Anton Anreith. Wine tastings and tours of the modern cellars are available, and there's a good restaurant in the old stables. From Groot Constantia it is a short walk to the Old Cape Farmstall, where delicious locally-grown fruit and vegetables, and home-made bread and cakes are sold.

The other two estates that make up Groot Constantia are **Klein Constantia** and **Buitenverwachting** (literally, "Beyond Expectations"), both on Klein Constantia Road. They're less formal than Groot Constantia, but just as pretty. Vin de Constance, a modern re-creation of the fine dessert wine so beloved by Napoléon, is sold at Klein Constantia, in a replica of the original bottle.

The Cape Town suburbs actually start further north, at Woodstock. Formerly a working-class Coloured area, this neighborhood is now attracting young professionals that buy and renovate its Victorian buildings. Observatory is bohemian, home to hippies and artists who frequent the local cafés and bars.

South Africa's most famous artist, Irma Stern (1894–1966), once lived at The Firs (Cecil Road, Rosebank), and this small house is now the excellent **Irma Stern Museum.** Stern's main claim to fame was that she introduced the European Expressionist concept to African art. The collection commemorates not only her own work, but also her overwhelming interest in the exotic, exhibiting items from her extensive travels. The fine **Baxter Theater Complex,** one of the most important centers for the arts in Cape Town, is also in Rosebank.

> Traffic lights are often referred to by their Afrikaans name, "robots."

Rondebosch, south of Rosebank, is distinguished by a number of particularly elegant 19th-century buildings, including the rather grand **University of Cape Town.** Cecil Rhodes built a great estate, Groote Schuur, which is now the official home of the President of South Africa. The legacy of the 19th-century prime minister can be seen in many of the street names throughout the area. On the slopes of Devil's Peak, off Rhodes Drive, are the stone steps and majestic sculpted lions leading to the **Rhodes Memorial,** styled after a Greek Temple. You can enjoy tremendous views of Cape Town from the Tea Garden, and zebra often graze nearby in an incongruous mix of African wildlife and 19th-century Colonial grandeur. Below the Memorial can be seen the thatched **Mostert's Mill,** built here in 1796 when the surrounding land was wheat fields.

Sports fans are drawn to the suburb of Newlands by **Norwich Park,** headquarters of the Western Province Cricket and Rugby Unions, and the site of international cricket and rugby matches. Newlands is also home to the **South African Rugby Museum** on Boundary Road, the largest rugby museum in the world. Exhibits date back to 1891, and it is a veri-

Commemorating 19th-century Prime Minister Cecil Rhodes, the Rhodes Memorial offers breathtaking views of the city.

table shrine to the national team, the Springboks. A working water mill, the **Josephine Mill,** is also on Boundary Road. Although it is now the office of the Cape Town Historical Society, the mill also still produces flour, and visitors can buy the flour and products made from it. The charming tea garden is the venue for concerts during the summer.

Shoppers head for plush Cavendish Square in Claremont, while horse-racing fans and socialites flock to Kenilworth Racecourse in nearby Kenilworth.

Wynberg means "wine mountain," and it was here that Jan Van Riebeeck planted the first vineyard in South Africa. The **Maynardville Open-Air Theater** puts on Shakespearean plays on summer evenings.

A drive through the suburbs makes you all-too-well aware of the great divide between rich and poor that still exists here. To the east lie the bleak expanses of the **Cape Flats** townships, where Africans and Coloureds inhabit their own separate areas in a painful legacy of South Africa's recent past. Life here is still harsh, all-too-frequently violent, and conditions squalid, yet visitors are often surprised and heartened by the positive attitude and courage of many of the inhabitants. Tourists wishing to explore the Cape Flats are firmly advised not to travel here alone. The only safe way is via one of the township tours (see page 115).

EXCURSIONS FROM CAPE TOWN

Another joy of Cape Town is the variety of tempting destinations close by, including the world-famous Garden Route and the Winelands. Whether you have just a day to spare, or the luxury of taking some longer breaks around the Western Cape, you'll be spoiled by the choices.

Cape Peninsula to Cape Point

A drive to the Cape of Good Hope, returning to Cape Town via the False Bay coast makes a superb full-day's excursion, incorporating glorious beaches, colorful fishing ports, stunning views of mountains and ocean, and a multitude of indigenous flora and fauna.

Take Beach Road out of the city center and head south, past the striped **Mouille Point Lighthouse,** the oldest in South Africa. Beach Road becomes Queens, then Victoria Road, winding along the hillside through Bantry Bay and Clifton, an area known locally as "Millionaires Row," boasting some of the most expensive homes in the country (see page 92).

After the family resort of Camps Bay, the shoreline opens up, giving good views of the coast, and the road runs along the foot of the Twelve Apostles. The shoreline south of here is popular with divers, and shipwrecks can be seen from the roadside. Further along, a roadside craft and curio market marks the turn to **Llandudno,** an elite, small village in an outstanding setting with a truly gorgeous beach.

Continue on Victoria Road to the fishing town of **Hout Bay.** Take time to wander around **Mariner's Wharf** complex, with its famed Fish Market and seafood restaurants, and one of the biggest selections of nautical souvenirs available anywhere. You can take a boat trip to see the seals and seabirds on Duiker Island, visit the **Hout Bay Museum,** or check out the thousands of noisy residents at the **World of Birds Wildlife Sanctuary.**

About 1 km (0.6 miles) further along the road past Mariner's Wharf you'll find an excellent fish and chip shop, Fish on the Rock. You can sit outside and enjoy wonderful views across Hout Bay to Chapmans Peak while chomping into fresh *snoek* or yellowtail and chips.

On the other side of the bay, high on a natural rock column near the shore at the start of Chapman's Peak Drive, stands a 1-m (5-ft) tall statue of a Cape leopard, a reminder of the days when the area was richer in wildlife. **Chapman's Peak Drive,**

On the road again… Chapman's Peak Drive is an unforgettable scenic experience from behind the wheel.

one of the most scenic routes in the Western Cape, winds along 10 km (6 miles) from Hout Bay to Noordhoek. In an extraordinary engineering exercise, it was carved out of the mountain face, and took seven years to build, opening in 1922. At its highest point it is 600 m (almost 2,000 ft) above the ocean, with breathtaking views down a sheer drop to the water below. A drive along it is an unforgettable experience, but there are few opportunities to stop.

Noordhoek is home to many artists, and from October to May it is possible to visit some of their studios along the Noordhoek Art Route.

The little hamlet of Kommetjie, lying at the end of a tidal lagoon, is hugely popular for watersports. Surfing competitions are often held at Long Beach, on which lies the wreck of a steamer that foundered during a storm in 1900. A detour along the M65 out of Kommetjie leads to the fascinating **Masephumelele Village,** a traditional Xhosa village, open to the public at weekends.

From Kommetjie, the drive to the holiday village of Scarborough passes high along the cliff tops. While en route keep an eye out for the baboons. At Scarborough the road heads south to Cape Point or over the mountains to Simon's Town. At this junction there is a wonderful craft stand selling magnificent wood carvings and stone statues, some over 3 m (almost 10 ft) in height.

The **Cape of Good Hope Nature Reserve** is 8,094 hectares (20,000 acres) of windswept natural beauty. It is home to over 1,000 species of indigenous flora, and in the spring hardy wildflowers brave gale force winds to provide a brilliant show of color. Wildlife includes the Cape mountain zebra, eland, and ostriches. Although the baboon population can look entertaining, repeated — and strictly forbidden — feeding from tourists has made them aggressive. There are strict rules governing the whole reserve, and officials are alert to those breaking the regulations.

Take care when hiking, as the vegetation is home to such snakes as cobras and puff-adders.

You can explore this magnificent reserve by car or on foot, and it is well worth it. At **Cape Point** a **Funicular Railway** runs from the Visitors Center to the **Cape Light.** There are truly spectacular views of the **Cape of Good Hope** and along the Cape. The water smashes against the rocks a dizzying distance below. The old lighthouse you can see was superseded in 1914 by a more powerful one, after the Portuguese liner was wrecked here. Marine life includes whales, dolphins, and seals. Blue- and yellow-fin tuna are fished in these waters. There is a fine restaurant with fantastic views across to Muizenberg and the False Bay coastline. There are also plenty of picnic and barbecue spots, and great walking along miles of unspoiled beaches.

On leaving the Reserve, head up the coast road towards **Simon's Town.** The home of the **South African Naval Museum,** it was once a major naval base and still has close links with the

service. Look out for the statue in Jubilee Square that pays tribute to a Great Dane dog, the mascot of British sailors based here during World War II. The **Black Marlin** seafood restaurant at Miller's Point is one of the best in the country, and the views from here are terrific. Children will love the **Warrior Toy Museum,** but the greatest attraction lies just

Atop Cape Light — coastal breeze, spectacular views, fine dining, and then some.

With all the action lining this bustling beach, can you believe Muizenburg was once the site of a fierce 18th-century battle?

south of the town, at **Boulders Beach.** This is the domain of black and white **jackass penguins.** One beach, home to the colony, is protected, but these delightful, charismatic birds venture onto the swimming beaches near the parking lot.

Traveling north along the coast road to Fish Hoek, you could briefly detour along Red Hill Road to the biggest gemstone polishing factory in the world, Topstones. Children enjoy climbing the great piles of stones, filling buckets to take home with them.

Fish Hoek is one of the best whale-watching spots along the Cape Peninsula. From **Jager's Walk,** a concrete walkway which runs towards Simon's Town, it is possible to get incredible views of these magnificent mammals from July to November. In 1927 ancient burial sites were discovered at Fish Hoek, in Peers Cave, the walls of which are covered in San rock paintings.

If you have time, head off-route along Kommetjie Road to **Silvermine Nature Reserve,** home to a great diversity of animals, birds, and plants. The reserve runs parallel to Kalk Bay, a lively fishing port, where you can buy fish literally straight off the brightly-painted boats.

Continuing east from Fish Hoek you come to **Muizenberg,** the scene of a fierce battle between the British and the Dutch in 1795. In the 1920s Muizenberg was the haunt of the rich and famous, many of whom built holiday homes here. The diverse architectural styles are fascinating, with fine Edwardian houses contrasting with fishermen's cottages, and colorful bathing huts line the beaches. Muizenberg Pavilion is popular with children, who enjoy the waterslide and camel rides. It is also the site of a Sunday morning flea market.

> It has become a West Coast tradition that any drivers spotting a tortoise in the road should stop, pick it up gently, and place it on the side of the road, out of harm's way.

In truth, Muizenberg is now rather seedy, but it still has plenty of interest. The **Natale Labia Museum** is a branch of the South African National Gallery, and many of the personal belongings of Cecil Rhodes can be seen at **Rhodes Cottage.** This simple, thatched building, once Rhodes's holiday home, is now a museum.

From Muizenberg, it is an easy drive up the M3, through the Southern Suburbs, back to the city center.

Stellenbosch and the Winelands

Within 30 minutes' drive of Cape Town along the N1 lie over 100 vineyards, where wine-tasting can be enjoyed in delightful surroundings. A tour of this scenic region is a visual delight as well as a joy for lovers of the grape. Enduring images visitors take home with them include white, gabled Cape Dutch houses and farm buildings set against the bright green of vines in full leaf, dwarfed by towering mountains. Fine restaurants, antique and gourmet food shops abound, while museums give a glimpse of Colonial rural life.

South Africa is the oldest non-European wine-producing country in the world, its wines respected the world over. The Western Cape is the key region, producing 4,000 individual wines from 315 vineyards. Stellenbosch and the surrounding area are the heart of the industry.

Jan Van Riebeeck planted the first vines in the country, but things really developed after Huguenot refugees arrived from France in the late 17th century, bringing their winemaking expertise with them.

All types of wine are made here, but the country is best known for its fabulous whites, and for Pinotage, a fruity, almost purple wine made from a unique cross between pinot noir and cinsaut grapes, first developed in Stellenbosch.

Very good wine can be bought for as little as R40 a bottle, with a few highly-enjoyable labels costing less. High interest rates make it uneconomic for estates to lay wine down, so you can buy a case or two of quite exceptional wine at a good price, and enjoy it at its finest five or ten years later.

The Stellenbosch Wine Route is the oldest and most famous of several established in recent years throughout the Winelands, each incorporating vineyards of varying sizes. All offer wine-tasting, and some have restaurants and shops, or will sell picnics to enjoy in the grounds. Following two or three routes, exploring their towns and attractions, can easily take the better part of a week. It is possible to experience many of the pleasures of the Winelands in a day, but taking two days and including an overnight stop can make for a thoroughly enjoyable and relaxing excursion. It is best to visit in summer, when the vines are in leaf, or at harvest time when they display their autumn foliage and there's plenty of activity.

Accommodation in this area is excellent, with many fine small country hotels and guest houses, often in beautiful old buildings, including the oldest country inn in South Africa, **D'Ouwe Werf** in Stellenbosch. Additionally, some vineyards offer overnight accommodation. At Delaire, the hillside cottages look right out onto the Franschhoek Valley.

First settled in 1679, **Stellenbosch** is the second oldest town in South Africa. It is now a busy university town, and no longer a pretty winelands village. Much of the charm has disappeared, but a walk around Stellenbosch is still rewarding. The numerous old oaks lining the streets resulted in the town's nickname "Eikestad," which means "oak town." **Dorp Street** contains some marvelous old buildings, including a fascinating shop which has changed little over the past century, becoming a tourist attraction in its own right: **Oom Samie Se** **Winkel** ("Uncle Sammy's Store") is packed with handmade

Simonsberg Mountain overlooks the nearly 30 estates that comprise the plush sprawl of the Stellenbosch Wine Route.

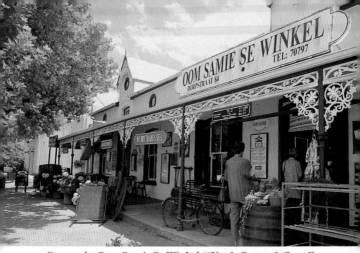

Stop on by Oom Samie Se Winkel ("Uncle Sammy's Store") for handmade crafts, antiques, fine foods, and local charm.

crafts, wines, basketry, dried fruit, antiques, lacework, and farm implements, and tea is served in the restaurant.

There are plenty of good shops in the town, and some lovely Cape Dutch, Georgian, and Victorian houses. The **Village Museum** on Ryneveld Street is a complex of historic houses, depicting in remarkable detail the life of the townsfolk over three centuries. Even the gardens are perfectly in period. The **Sasol Art Museum** is home to the University of Stellenbosch's art collection, and also has displays of prehistoric artifacts. The **Stellenryck Wine Museum** in Strand Street covers the history of winemaking, while for the children there is the fascinating **Toy and Miniature Museum** in an old rectory at the corner of Market and Herte Streets, next to the Tourist Office.

The **Stellenbosch Wine Route** includes nearly 30 estates. Those closest to Stellenbosch include the following:

Blaauwklippen, with its thatched manor house and coach museum, where visitors can take rides on some of the old carts and gigs on display; **Morgenhof,** at the foot of the Simonsberg mountains, which produces outstanding wines from its beautiful estate, including Merlot and Cabernet Sauvignon; and **Spier** — one of the vineyards most geared-up to entertain visitors. It boasts the famed Jonkershuis Restaurant, offers pony rides, and holds concerts at its open-air amphitheater. A section of the estate has been given over to a conservation group that has used it to house a family of hand-reared cheetahs, and visitors can stroke these beautiful spotted creatures. One of the smallest and oldest wineries, **Kanonkop,** has an exceptional range of award-winning wines, renowned world-wide.

From its restored Cape homestead of Vlottenburg, on the R310 southwest from Stellenbosch, **Wineways** offers "the whole Cape experience under one roof," with a multimedia big-screen presentation in the Discovery Centre. Wine tastings are offered here, and wine can be shipped worldwide.

The R310 northeast from Stellenbosch towards Franschhoek takes you through the stunning Helshoogte Pass, and some of the most beautiful scenery in the Winelands. Head up to the "vineyard in the sky," **Delaire.** From here, the view of the Simonsberg Mountain and across the Franschhoek Valley is memorable, particularly at sunset. **Boschendal,** an estate on the other side of the Pass, just before the junction with the R45, combines the opportunity to sample excellent red wines with a tour of a magnificent Cape Dutch manor, furnished in spectacular 17th- and 18th-century style.

Franschhoek, set in a valley with mountains on three sides, is the culinary showpiece of the Western Cape. With some 30 restaurants offering outstanding Cape Malay and Provençale cuisine, it has become a popular place for fashionable Capetonians to wine and dine, and booking ahead is essential.

This pretty village is everything you'd imagine it to be. It was founded in 1680 by Huguenots who came over from France. Their story is told in detail at the **Huguenot Memorial Museum** on Lambrecht Street. The **Huguenot Monument,** also on Lambrecht Street, pays tribute to these French settlers.

A number of vineyards can be reached on foot from the village, with the majority lying off Huguenot and Main roads. At **Cabrière Estate,** off the Franschhoek Pass, renowned winemaker Achim von Arnim demonstrates the art of *sabrage,* slicing the neck of a bottle of sparkling wine with a sabre. The cellar at **Mont Rochelle** is decorated with stained-glass and chandeliers, and there's a stud farm and guest house at **Chamonix.**

The R303 leads northwest from Franschhoek to **Paarl,** the largest winelands town, home to the **KWV,** the giant wine-growing co-operative. The KWV's 22-hectare (54-acre) cellar complex here is the largest in the world, featuring the awe-inspiring Cathedral Cellar, with a barrel-vaulted roof.

Paarl is rather industrialized now and has lost its charm, but has two main claims to historical significance. Here, in 1875, the Afrikaans language was first officially recognized, a fact commemorated by the **Taal** ("language") **Monument** on the hill above the town, and by the **Afrikaans Taal Museum** on Pastorie Street. It is also the closest town to **Victor Verster Prison,** where Nelson Mandela spent the final years of his 27-year incarceration.

A much-respected ceramic artist, Clementina Van der Walt, has her studio on Langenhoven Street, and the weavers at the Ikhweze Center handmake rugs and garments using mohair.

Le Bonheur Crocodile Farm on the Babylonstoren Road is home to over 1,000 of the reptiles, selling their meat and products made from their skins. There's a fine bird sanctuary along the Berg River, and a number of ostrich farms. The delicate *waterblommetjies* (waterlilies), an essential ingredient of a traditional Cape Malay stew, are picked by workers wading in waist-deep water at Schoongezicht.

Vineyards near Paarl include **Fairview,** with its herd of Saanen goats who live in a tall stone tower, climbing up its spiraling ramp to reach the entrance. Fairview produces fine wines, but is also known

> Gasoline (petrol) can usually only be paid for in cash.

for its excellent goat's milk cheeses. The balcony of the tasting room at **Laborie** looks across the vineyards to Paarl Mountain, and there is a beautiful rose garden.

From Paarl, you can drive back to Cape Town along the N1, or head towards Worcester for an overnight stop preceding an excursion to the Breede River Valley and the Little Karoo. You can enjoy fabulous views from the Du Toitskloof Pass, part of R101, the old road which runs from Paarl to Worcester reaching over 800 m (2640 ft) at its highest. The Drakenstein Lion Park, off R101, is home to three packs of lions. These "Kings of Africa" can be viewed from an overhead walkway. The faster route from Paarl to Worcester is through the Huguenot Toll Tunnel, but you'll miss some good views if you take this option.

The Breede River Valley and Little Karoo

The **Breede River Valley** is the largest fruit and wine-producing area in the Western Cape. Its principal town, Ceres, was named after the Roman goddess of fertility. The road from Worcester leads across this heavily-cultivated region to the **Little Karoo** (*Klein Karoo*), an area rich in haunting San rock art, and packed with ostrich farms. En route it passes wheatlands, vineyards, orchards, majestic mountains, and small towns, their streets bright with the fragile, lilac-colored flowers of **jacaranda** trees. Though not as famous as the Garden Route, this mountain journey is one of the most scenic and dramatic in the Western Cape.

The Worcester vineyards produce about 25% of South African wines. The most interesting thing to see is the **Kleinplasie Open-Air Museum** (off Robertson Road). The life of pioneer Cape farmers is depicted in a "living" museum, where workers in period costume milk cows, bake bread in outdoor ovens, tread grapes, make candles, shoe horses, and distill fiery home-made brandy.

More than 80 species of crocodiles, snakes, and turtles live next door, at **Kleinplasie Reptile World,** while the **Karoo National Botanical Garden** on Roux Street features acres of the fascinating succulents that grow in the semi-desert of the Little Karoo.

From Worcester you could head northwest on R43, past the towering Hex River Mountains and along the glorious Bain's Kloof Pass to **Tulbagh.** A devastating earthquake in 1969 destroyed many of this small 18th-century town's oldest buildings, and what you see on Church Street is the culmination of years of meticulous restoration. The result is startling. Thirty-two of the houses have been either rebuilt or given new frontages, but it's impossible to spot where the new and old meet. The story of the earthquake is told in the four restored buildings which form the **Oude Kerk Volksmuseum.** Another Tulbagh attraction is **Paddagang.** The name of this early 19th-century restaurant means "frog house," and all the labels on the wine sold here feature frogs.

To experience the Little Karoo, head southeast from Worcester, along the N15 to Robertson, an important horse-breeding area, and on to **Montagu.** This elegant Victorian town, set amidst mighty mountains, contains some wonderful houses, no less than 22 of which are national monuments,

All but leveled by a 1969 earthquake, Tulbagh has regained its picture-perfect allure through years of careful restoration.

with 14 on Long Street alone. You can relax and revive your-self with a soak in the hot mineral springs at the Montagu Springs Resort, or hike or take a 4WD into the Langeberg Mountains, revered by rock climbers. A popular outing here, unique to the area, is a tractor and trailer ride to the summit of the Langeberg, followed by a traditional South African meal.

From Montagu, the R62 winds through the mountains across the Little Karoo. This arid landscape is enigmatic. At some times of the day or the year it looks barren and lifeless, save for the odd ostrich. At others the light catches the mountains, transforming all you see.

En route you pass through the village of Calitzdorp, at the foot of the craggy Huis River Pass. This region produces wonderful dried fruits, and you will pass many roadside stalls selling these, plus fresh produce.

Oudtshoorn, founded on ostrich farming, is "the ostrich capital of the world." The dry climate of the Karoo is ideal for breeding these large, flightless birds, and their favorite food grows well here. It is impossible to travel around the region without seeing flocks of them. Though once farmed for feathers, they are now farmed primarily for their low-cholesterol meat, but ostrich leather is also becoming fashionable for clothes and shoes, and their eggs are good to eat, and painted and sold as souvenirs.

The story of this industry, which enjoyed a glorious heyday from the 1880s until World War I, is chronicled at the excellent **C.P. Net Museum** on Baron Van Rheede Street.

Many ostrich farms are open to the public. **Highgate** (off Mossel Bay Road) was the first to exploit the tourism poten-

---

"Feather Millionaires"

Towards the end of the 19th century, the demand for ostrich plumes for the hats and feather boas of the ladies of fashion was unprecedented. Prices soared as ostrich feathers became a commodity of enormous value, and, as a consequence, many ostrich farmers around Oudtshoorn became millionaires virtually overnight.

These "feather millionaires" threw themselves enthusiastically into the extravagant lifestyle their newfound wealth bought them. Their excesses rivaled those of the Randlords of Johannesburg, who had made countless millions from gold and diamonds.

They built themselves elaborate sandstone mansions, known as "feather palaces," splendid examples of which can be seen in Oudtshoorn today. Many of these were an unfortunate combination of lavish spending and questionable taste. The **Le Roux Townhouse** on High Street is a restored example of one of the greatest of these mansions. Visitors to the **Safari Ostrich Farm** on the R328 can visit Welgeluk, another "feather palace."

When ostrich feathers fell out of fashion at the start of World War I, the market crashed spectacularly, reducing many of the "feather millionaires" to poverty.

tial of ostrich farming. Here you can see the birds hatch, hold the chicks, watch the adults being plucked, and even go for a ride. Ostrich racing is a popular local entertainment, though the exhibition of racing here is disappointing. You can also eat ostrich meat or buy products made from the leather.

Oudtshoorn is 500 km (310 miles) east of Cape Town, but just 63 km (39 miles) north of Wilderness on the coast, so it makes an ideal stop-over point before a journey along the Garden Route.

One of Oudtshoorn's feathered natives — find out how they made millionaires overnight!

Three km (2 miles) north of Oudtshoorn is the **Cango Wildlife Ranch.** This breeding center for rare animals is a fantastic place to see African wildlife, including lions, jaguars, crocodiles, snakes, meerkats, tortoises and wallabies. Visitors are allowed to meet the more approachable residents, and it is an unforgettable experience to encounter playful young cheetahs.

Twenty-nine km (18 miles) further north along the R328 are the spectacular **Cango Caves.** In 1780 a local farmer discovered this sequence of vast, ancient caverns, linked by narrow passages under the Swartberg Mountains. Over the past 100,000 years, water oozing through rock and limestone has resulted in an intricate underground landscape of stalactites and dripstone formations that is simply breathtaking.

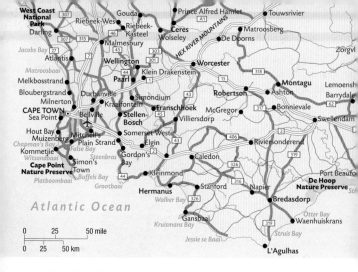

Garden Route

With the exception of Table Mountain, the Garden Route is the best-known tourist destination on the Western Cape. Though its name conjures up visions of an area abundant in floral splendor, many visitors are surprised to find that it is more forest than garden. The title "Garden Route" reflects the lush vegetation covering the rolling hills lying between the dramatic Tsitsikamma mountains and the breathtaking shoreline of the Indian Ocean, home to whales and dolphins.

This is a popular resort area for South African vacationers and can become very congested during their main holiday season. Increasing over-development to meet the demand of the tourists has resulted in the inevitable loss of some of the natural beauty, and to many the Garden Route will be a disappointment. However, there are still many unspoiled jewels to enjoy.

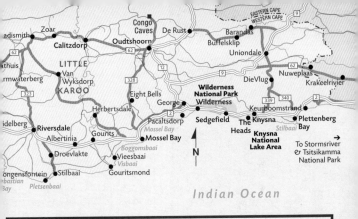

The Winelands & The Garden Route

The Garden Route is often thought to stretch the 800 km (497 miles) from Cape Town to Port Elizabeth, but actually begins at Mossel Bay, some 400 km (248 miles) east of Cape Town, and ends at Storms River, about 190 km (118 miles) further east. This is covered by the excellent N2, but to truly experience the natural wealth of the area, head off the main road and take in some of the picturesque older roads through attractive coastal towns and past exquisite lakes, lagoons, and rivers.

The area has numerous signposts, so it is easy to wander off-route and then return to the N2 again. You can reach Knysna on a lengthy day trip from Cape Town, but this won't allow you time to see very much. It is advisable to allow at least two days, with an overnight stop, if you really want an enduring memory to take home with you.

When you see the industrial approach to **Mossel Bay,** don't be put off. The center of the town is charming. The **Bartolomeu**

Dias Museum Complex is well worth a visit, so take time to wander around. In its grounds you'll find the great Post Office Tree, by which sailors used to leave letters for passing ships.

The seashells from around the world, in the adjacent **Shell Museum,** are quite lovely, while the Aquarium provides a fascinating chance to see living shellfish in their natural habitat. The swimming from Santos Beach is among the best on the Garden Route. A cruise around Seal Island will allow you to spot comical jackass penguins and seals, as well as the great white sharks who feed on them. A walk through the Dana Bay Nature Reserve leads to St. Blaize Lighthouse.

Take a ride on the Outeniqua Choo Tjoe steam train — an easy way to enjoy the coast.

Twice a day, the **Outeniqua Choo Tjoe** steam-train travels the 30 km (18.5 miles) scenic journey between the town of George (65 km/40 miles east of Mossel Bay) and Knysna. There can be few more relaxing ways to view one of the most beautiful stretches of Cape coastline than from the carriages of this little engine. Just north of the N2 near Glentana is Hoogekraal, the old homestead of the family of former South African premier, P.W. Botha. It is now a country guest house. The antique-laden building is steeped in history, entertainingly recounted at the candlelit dinners hosted by the owners.

Eighteen km (11 miles) on from George, the N2 bisects **Wilderness.** Lavish holiday homes now sprawl along the dunes bordering the famed long beach of what was once a small, romantic village.

The village of Wilderness marks the start of the **Wilderness National Park.** This wetlands area with its lush forests, covers over 2,500 hectares (6,177 acres), stretching 28 km (17.5 miles) along the coastline to Sedgefield, and incorporating 15 km (just over 9 miles) of inland waterways including five rivers and five lakes. It is the natural habitat for 250 species of birds, including 79 different types of waterfowl. There are a number of marked hiking trails, and it is also possible to explore the area from the water in rented canoes. In the spring, it is vibrant with multicolored carpets of wildflowers.

Just after Sedgefield, a right turn towards Buffel's Bay leads to an unexpected gem; a glorious, undeveloped beach bordering the **Goukamma Nature and Marine Reserve.** The beach is virtually deserted, bathers preferring the more sheltered waters of Buffel's Bay itself, just 1 km (0.6 miles) further on. Goukamma covers over 200 sq km (124 square miles), including Groenvlei, a freshwater lake very popular with anglers. Rich wildlife includes fish eagles, rare African black oystercatchers, vervet monkeys, otters, and mongoose. Marine life is equally plentiful; dolphins are often seen. During the breeding season (July–November), southern right whales pass by on their migration route.

Knysna, 102 km (63 miles) east of Mossel Bay, and a five-hour drive along the N2 from Cape Town, is one of the main tourist destinations along the Garden Route. It is a convenient place to stay, but has lost its charm in the scramble to cash in on tourism. It looks scruffy, and the arrival of a McDonald's in the Main Street will do nothing to improve this. There are no beaches, but the town is in an attractive hilly setting on the shores of the tidal Knysna Lagoon. The Heads (two steep sandstone cliffs) and a coral reef guard the sea mouth of the lagoon. A cruise to the Heads from Knysna Quay is a popular excursion, with ferry tickets available through the tourist information bureau.

The history of the town, which grew to prosperity on the timber trade that nearly destroyed its massive hardwood forests, is told at the **Knysna Museum** on Main Street, in a building which also houses South Africa's first Angling Museum.

To experience the **Diepwalle Forest** take the R339, a well-maintained unpaved road. Though a shadow of its former self, the forest is still impressive. If you're lucky, you'll glimpse a Knysna Lourie bird amongst the huge, centuries-old stinkwood and yellowwood trees that form a thick canopy overhead. There is a marked Elephant Trail, and traffic signs warn of elephant crossing. Unfortunately the elephants are no longer here — the few remaining pachyderms were relocated to the Shamwari Game Reserve, 300 km (186 miles) east of the town, and now the only way to see them is at Knysna Elephant Park. Some of the elephants here are so tame you can feed and hug them.

It is possible to buy finely-crafted items, made from the Forest hardwoods, from the talented artists that sell their works in the street markets and craft shops along Main Street, and at the roadside stalls along the Garden Route from Knysna to Plettenberg Bay.

Knysna is lively at night, and has many good restaurants. If you're partial to oysters you'll be in your element here — Knysna is home to one of the largest oyster farms in the world.

Thirty km (18 miles) east lies **Plettenberg Bay,** a beautiful spot spoiled only by the hideous modern hotel built near the beach. It's a fashionable resort with safe bathing, and consequently gets very crowded in high summer.

The bay is formed by the Robberg Peninsula and Keurbooms Strand, and is home to some wonderful marine life. Robberg is a nature reserve, named after the seals who live at the base of the cliffs. A walk to the very end of the peninsula will take about four hours.

A large number of dolphins make Plettenberg Bay their home year-round. Boat trips around the bay run from the beach, and Ocean Adventures (Tel. 04453/35083) runs a particularly informative excursion. The experience of being in a small boat with dolphins playing in the waves, so close that you could touch them, is truly incredible. Between July and November there is also a good chance of seeing whales, and the Whale Hotline gives updates on their presence (Tel. 04457/33743).

If parts of the Garden Route are disappointing, **Tsitsikamma National Park** is the opposite. This strikingly beautiful reserve encompasses hardwood forests, sparkling pools, coral reefs, dunes, long stretches of sandy beach with safe swimming spots, deep gorges, waterfalls, and the Otter Trail, one of the most popular hikes in the country. The world's highest bungee jump is here. Those adventurous enough to leap off Bloukrans Bridge have a 216-m (708-ft) fall before they are snapped back up again by the bungee.

At **Storms River Mouth,** within Tsitsikamma, the Garden Route ends in a spectacular fashion. Cliffs covered in dense forest lead down to black rocks against which waves crash violently. You can walk along the boardwalk from the restaurant at Storms River Rest Camp, past the cave inhabited thousands of years ago by strandlopers (beachcombers), and gaze down at the surging waters of the river mouth from the Paul Sauer suspension bridge.

Hermanus and the Tip of Africa

The best land-based whale-watching in the world is to be found around **Hermanus,** just an hour's drive from Cape Town. A day-trip to this seaside resort can be immensely rewarding, with

cliff viewpoints as little as 30 m away (98 ft) from these spectacular mammals.

The excitement is nearly tangible; reports of sightings draw
crowds who flock to the shore to watch in wonder. Hermanus
can become very crowded, but the glorious sight runs right
around from Betty's Bay in the east to the coast off the De
Hoop Nature Reserve, and there are plenty of excellent viewing spots along the route.

When it's not whale season, this region is still well-worth
visiting, as it combines many of the best aspects of the Western
Cape in one relatively compact area. If you have more than a
day to spare, a tour of this memorable stretch of coastline can
be combined with the Garden Route or Little Karoo.

Gentle Giants

From June to December, the waters around the Western
Cape host some rare visitors; migrating whales who breed
and calve in sheltered bays along the coastline.

For several months whale calves can be seen swimming
and playing with their mothers. This joyous display is truly
unforgettable. Peak viewing time is August to November,
and many towns along the route hold annual Whale Festivals to welcome these gentle giants.

Humpback and Bryde's whales can be spotted, but the
most common sightings are of southern right whales. With
tragic irony, the ages-old, instinctive breeding journey of
these magnificent mammals nearly brought about their extinc-
tion. Southern right whales were so named because they
were the "right" quarry for whalers. Every bit of these slow-
moving mammals could be used, and conveniently, they
floated when dead, making retrieval of the bodies easy.
Over 12,000 were killed in these waters. Now protected,
the population is increasing at a rate of 7% per year.

Hermanus lies 110 km (68 miles) from Cape Town on the shores of Walker Bay. The quickest route from the city is via the N2, over Sir Lowry's Pass, with its stunning views down to False Bay, then via R43. Two km (1 mile) before Hermanus, you come to R320 (the sign reads "to Caledon). A detour up here leads to three **vineyards,** Whale Haven, Hamilton Russell, and Bouchard Finlayson. Walker Bay wines are amongst the most respected in South Africa, and Hamilton Russell's are some of the most expensive in the country. If this is the only excursion you're making from Cape Town, you could make an earlier detour, off the N2 at Somerset West, to exquisite **Vergelegen,** one of the most beautiful wine estates in South Africa.

An alternative route to Hermanus is to head 50 km (31 miles) out of Cape Town on the N2, then take R44. The renowned **Harold Porter National Botanical Garden** at Betty's Bay has more than 1,600 species of fynbos. The wildlife here is elusive, but includes baboons and leopards. Nearby **Stoney Point** rivals Hermanus for whale-watching, and is home to a colony of jackass penguins. R44 takes you through Kleinmond, a village with safe swimming off of a broad, crescent-shaped beach; to R43; and to Hermanus.

Originally a fishing and whaling village, Hermanus is now a popular resort, but the whales continue to contribute to the town's finances; now through tourism. The **Old Harbour Museum** tells the story of the whaling industry, and the mysterious and soothing songs of the whales out at sea are caught by sonar buoy and transmitted live into the museum.

Hermanus is home to the world's only **Whale Crier,** who strides through the streets, announcing whale sightings on his unique kelp horn. He can be contacted; Tel. (083) 212 1075. A toll-free Whale Hotline (Tel. 0800/228 8222) also keeps would-be watchers updated.

From Hermanus, head east inland, past vast fields of barley to Bredasdorp. The town has some fine old Cape Dutch buildings, but the **Shipwreck Museum,** with relics recovered from this region's notorious waters, is a tourist favorite.

Forty-five km (28 miles) south of Bredastorp is **Cape Agulhas,** a small town with striking, multi-colored roofs that lies at the southernmost point of Africa. It is here, and not at the Cape of Good Hope, as is often thought, that the Indian and Atlantic oceans meet. This spot is marked by a cairn a short distance from **Agulhas Lighthouse.** If there is any place on earth where you'd expect to see dramatic cliffs, it would be here. However, this mighty continent disappointingly slopes gently into the oceans — next stop, Antarctica. Nearby Struisbaai boasts an immaculate 14-km (8-mile) beach; the longest uninterrupted stretch of white sandy beach in Southern Africa.

East of Cape Agulhas lies the idyllic village of **Arniston,** named after a ship wrecked here in 1815. Locals call it Waenhuiskrans, after an enormous cavern eroded into the cliffs close to the village. The landscape here is simply stunning. Near the harbor, historic thatched fishermen's cottages look over a turquoise sea with rolling white sand dunes in the distance.

The **De Hoop Nature Reserve,** further along the coast, is unforgettable. Fifteen km (9 miles) north of Arniston, it is reached by returning to Bredasdorp, then taking a well-marked dirt road. The reserve has 50 km (30 miles) of spectacular coastline, flanked by pristine white sand dunes, rising as high as 90 m (295 ft). This stretch of water is the breeding ground for most of the Cape's whales. Rich wildlife includes bontebok, Cape Mountain Zebra, and over 250 different species of birds, and an extraordinary variety of fynbos grow here. There are self-catering cottages on site, and a stop-over at De Hoop is an alternative to Arniston, before heading north through the fine old town of Swellendam.

For the best land-based whale watching in the world, be sure to stop off at the seaside splendor of Hermanus.

The West Coast and Cederberg

The 400-km (248-mile) stretch of land north of Cape Town that forms the West Coast is an area of diverse beauty. It lacks the lushness of the Garden Route or the Winelands, but its attractions are considerable. The Atlantic Ocean bestows on this region a wild coastline, a rich harvest of seafood, huge and varied communities of seabirds, and the awe-inspiring spectacle of migrating whales. Inland, the rugged Cederberg mountains form its eastern border, their fascinating rock formations a natural sculptor's gallery. Ancient San rock paintings speak of human life here long before the arrival of the first Europeans, and a wealth of wildlife can be seen. Between mountains and ocean lie the wheatfields and vineyards of the Swartland, and wildflowers carpet this whole region in a springtime display of extraordinary vibrancy.

On a day-long excursion from Cape Town, you can travel along R27, visiting the interesting town of Darling, and the West Coast National Park. Alternatively, you could head straight for the Cederberg Wilderness Area, and view San rock paintings and remarkable natural rock sculptures. A longer excursion of two to three days would accommodate a loop right around this wild region.

Just ten minutes outside of Cape Town on R27 is the resort of **Bloubergstrand,** with its unrivalled view of Table Mountain, seen across Table Bay.

The small town of **Darling** lies further along R27, 70 km (43 miles) north of Cape Town. Its many attractions include handsome old buildings and a Butter Museum. The annual spring flower show, held annually since 1917, is a major event. Darling is something of an artists' colony, and is also "home" to "Evita Bezuidenhout," the most famous character created by South Africa's hugely popular comedian and satirist, Pieter-Dirk Uys.

Like a scene from a Hitchcock movie, Bird Island is ruled by flocks of gannets, cormorants, and jackass penguins.

Nearby Yzerfontein is renowned for the sweet-tasting crayfish caught in its waters.

The wetlands of the **West Coast National Park** attract millions of waterfowl who make a safe home on its islands, away from ocean predators. Waders, pelicans, black oystercatchers, and flamingos can all be seen around **Langebaan Lagoon.** At the southern tip of the park is the **Potsberg Nature Reserve,** one of the closest areas to Cape Town for viewing spring wildflowers.

Further along R27 lies St. Helena Bay, where Vasco da Gama landed in 1497 during his voyage to discover the Spice Route. A simple stone monument commemorates the landing, and the story is told at the **Da Gama Museum.**

Two hours north of St. Helena Bay, mostly over dirt roads, the fishing port of **Lambert's Bay** is dominated by the huge colonies of seabirds at **Bird Island,** 100 m (328 ft) off shore. You can walk out along the seawall to the island, where the masses of noisy Cape gannets, cormorants, and jackass penguins can be seen from a special viewing tower. Boat trips operate from Lambert's Bay to view visiting whales (July–November), and year-round you can catch a glimpse of Cape fur seals, penguins, and dolphins. Schools of over 1,000 dolphins have been spotted.

Driving some 60 km (37 miles) east along R364 brings you to the northern tip of the Cederberg mountains and the **Cederberg Wilderness Area.** Time and the elements have eroded the sandstone into a surreal landscape that stretches as far as the eye can see. The most extraordinary shapes are in the south of the reserve. They include the **Wolfberg Arch,** a 30-m- (98-ft-) high natural archway of rock, and the **Maltese Cross,** a 22-m- (66-ft-) tall pillar.

Vegetation includes wild olives, purple-blue *ridderspoor*, the rare snow protea, and *rooibos* (see page 101). The region is named after the Clanwilliam cedar tree, which grows against cliffs, overhanging at altitudes of more than 1000 m

(3,280 ft) above sea level. Wildlife includes baboons, porcupine, aardvark, lynx, Cape fox, mongoose, and leopard. Puff adders and black spitting cobras inhabit the undergrowth, and Clanwilliam yellowfish swim in the Olifants River, named after the great herds of elephants once roamed on the vast planes to the south of the mountains.

This region was a favorite hunting ground of San bushmen for thousands of years. Their **rock paintings** remain throughout the area, notably in the beautiful private wilderness area of Bushmans Kloof. Here, on guided walks, you hear their history and interpretation. A few remaining San families used to live at the Kagga Kamma reserve, but they have recently moved back to the Kalahari.

Surreal rock formations along the Cederberg Mountains decorate the African skyline.

Clanwilliam is a good base from which to explore this area. There is plenty of accommodation, a museum, and, of course, rooibos tea.

Cape Town is about three hours' drive down the N7, past Citrusdal, a major citrus-producing town, and the giant, golden wheatfields of Swartland. En route, take care to avoid tortoises making valiant efforts to cross the road, and look to the horizon for a long-distance view of Table Mountain.

Essentials

In the following listing, "children" denotes age 14 and under, unless otherwise noted.

Castle of Good Hope, *Castle Street; Tel. (021) 469 1111.* Open 9am–4pm Mon–Sat. Admission R12. Free guided tours every hour, Feb–Nov, and every 30 minutes in Dec and Jan.

Groote Kerk, *Adderley Street and Church Square; Tel. (021) 461 7044.* Free. Free guided tours 10am– 2pm weekdays.

South African Cultural History Museum, *Adderley Street; Tel. (021) 461 8280.* Open Mon–Sat 9:30am–4pm. Adults R5, children R1

Houses of Parliament, *Parliament Street; Tel. (021) 403 2460/1/2.* Tickets to watch parliamentary sessions (Jan–June), are available from the Parliamentary Public Relations Section in the Old Assembly Wing. Free. Free one-hour guided tours run from July–Jan, operating at 11am and 2pm Mon–Thurs, and 11am only on Fri. Tickets should be booked in advance.

South African Library, *Company's Gardens; Tel. (021) 424 6320.* Open 9am–6pm Mon–Fri, and 9am–1pm Sat. Free.

South African Museum, *Company's Gardens; Tel. (021) 424 3330.* Open daily 10am–5pm. Adults R5, free to children, free to all on Wed.

Planetarium, *Company's Gardens; Tel. (021) 424 3330.* Open daily 10am–5pm. R7 adults, R8 in the evening; children R5.

South African National Gallery, *Government Avenue; Tel. (021) 465 1628.* Open 10am–5pm, Tues–Sun. Free.

Jewish Museum, *Hatfield Street; Tel. (021) 465 1546.* Open 1:30pm–5pm Tues and Thurs and 10:30am–noon Sun. Free.

Sendinggestig Museum, *Long Street; Tel. (021) 423 6755.* Open 9am–4pm, Mon–Fri and 9am–12 noon, Sat. Free.

Koopmans de Wet House, *35 Strand Street; Tel. (021) 424 2473.* Open 9:30am–4:30pm Tues–Sat. Adults R3, children R1.

Old Town House, *Greenmarket Square; Tel. (021) 424 6367.* Open daily 10am–5pm. R3 donation requested.

Bo-Kaap Museum, *71 Wale Street; Tel. (021) 424 3846*. Open 9:30am–4:30pm, Mon–Sat. Adults R3, children R1; free on Fri.

District Six Museum, *Buitenkant Methodist Church, 25a Buitenkant Street; Tel. (021) 461 8745*. Open Mon–Sat 10am–4pm and Sun by appointment. Donation requested.

Table Mountain Cableway, *Lower Cable Station, Tafelberg Road; Tel. (021) 242 5148*. Cable cars run every day, weather permitting, leaving Lower Cable Station every 15 minutes from 8am–9:30pm in Nov and late Jan through late Apr, 7am–10:30 pm Dec–late Jan, and 8:30am–5:30pm May–Oct. Adults R65 (round trip), children R35 through Apr; ticket prices beyond Apr unavailable at presstime.

South African National Maritime Museum, *Dock Road; Tel. (021) 419 2505*. Open 10am–5pm daily. Adults R10, children R3; charge includes entry to S.A.S. Somerset.

Two Oceans Aquarium, *V&A Waterfront; Tel. (021) 418 3823*. Open daily 9.30am–6pm. Adults R34, children (4–14) R18; children under four admitted free.

Telkom Exploratorium, *V&A Waterfront; Tel. (021) 419 5957*. Open 9am–6pm daily. Adults R10, children (4–17) R5; children under four admitted free.

Robben Island; *Museum Tel. (021) 409 5100. Official ferry service Tel. (021) 419 1300*. Ferries depart from Berties Landing at the V&A Waterfront on the hour from 9am–3pm weekdays and 9am–4pm on weekends and public holidays. Adults R100, students/senior citizens R70, children (4–14) R50. Fee includes boat trip.

Kirstenbosch National Botanical Gardens; *Tel. (021) 762 1166*. Open 365 days a year, from 8am–6pm Apr–Aug, and 8am–7pm Sept–Mar. Adults R7, children R3.

Groot Constantia, *Constantia; Tel. (021) 794 5067*. Museum open daily 10am–5pm. Adults R5, children R1.

Irma Stern Museum, *Cecil Road, Rosebank; Tel. (021) 685 5686*. Open 10am–5pm Tues–Sat. Adults R5, children R2.50.

South African Rugby Museum, *Boundary Road, Newlands; Tel. (021) 685 3038*. Open 9am–3pm daily. Free.

WHAT TO DO

SHOPPING

What to Buy

Arts and crafts from all over Africa can be bought in Cape Town. These vary in quality, but it is not difficult to find really beautifully made items at relatively low cost. Traditional West African **carved wooden masks,** made to celebrate events such as a birth or wedding, make a fascinating souvenir. Other African objects to look out for include **soapstone carvings,** intricate **beadwork,** colorful **fabrics, basket work,** and **wooden bowls.**

Gold, diamonds and other gems both precious and semi-precious are readily available, sometimes at incredibly low prices, and there are many talented jewelry designers working in the region. For a little fun, visit a gemstone "scratch patch," such as the one at the V&A Waterfront, where you can search for semi-precious stones in giant containers, then buy them by weight.

Colonial **antiques,** including porcelain, glassware, furniture, and jewelry, are also much in evidence, as are contemporary art, leather goods, and ceramics. You'll also see brightly-painted **ostrich eggs,** and bags, wallets, belts, and shoes made from ostrich skin.

Few travelers return from Cape Town without at least one bottle of the fine **wine** for which the region is renowned, and tasting before you buy is all part of the fun. Many vineyards and wine shops will arrange to ship your purchase to your home.

Where to Shop

The Golden Acre shopping mall in Adderley Street, and St. George's Mall, contain dozens of shops, including curio stores, and clothes, jewelry, and gift shops. Long Street is a

particularly good source of second-hand books and antique clothing.

Although there are numerous shops selling African arts and crafts, you'll generally find the same items in markets at much lower prices. Brightly-colored African fabrics abound at the flea market at Grand Parade, as do hand-crafted clothes, which you could also find at Greenmarket Square. The market at Kirstenbosch National Botanical Gardens (last Sunday of every month, September–May) is notable for the quality crafts on offer.

Choose from an amalgam of local hand-crafted goods at Greenmarket Square.

If you want to find everything in one place, head for the V&A Waterfront. Its Victoria and Alfred Mall and Victoria Wharf Shopping Centre contain hundreds of shops selling everything imaginable, and the huge Waterfront Craft Market is a fantastic source of high-quality items. Craftsmen can be seen at work in the Red Shed Craft Workshop in Victoria Wharf, and will custom-make items to the customer's specification.

In the charming small towns along the Cape Peninsula you'll find lots of local crafts and art, often of a very high standard, some sold from roadside stalls. Hout Bay and Noordhoek are known for their artists, sculptors, and potters, while the Mariner's Wharf at Hout Bay boasts a shop specializing in maritime memorabilia, including shipwreck relics. Kalk Bay and Simon's Town are particularly well endowed with shops selling unusual gifts and art objects, and there's a regular craft market at Hermanus.

Many of the wineries sell not only their own wine, but also gifts and/or gourmet foods. The towns along the Wine Routes can also be a good source of Cape Dutch collectables and antiques. The Winelands Craft Market is held every Sunday in the summer in Stellenbosch, which also has lots of curio shops in the old town, and Paarl has a Art and Craft Market on the first Saturday of each month. If you travel to Stellenbosch, don't miss Oom Samie se Winkel in Dorp Street. This remarkable emporium has remained virtually unchanged over the past 100 years, and is full of fascinating items.

The largest shopping center in the Cape is Tygervalley, in the northern suburbs. The main shopping complex in the southern suburbs is Claremont's Cavendish Square. This region is the center of South Africa's garment industry, and Salt River and Woodstock have many factory outlets where it is possible to find bargains.

ENTERTAINMENT

Surprisingly, for such a cosmopolitan city, Cape Town doesn't boast the sophisticated nightlife of Johannesburg, but there's still plenty to do after dark.

Theater and Live Music

Local theater is extremely good, with top-class classical opera, ballet, drama, and satirical reviews to be seen at the home of the Cape Performing Arts Board, the Nico Theater in the city center. The Baxter Theater in Rosebank presents contemporary music and dance.

If your taste is for more traditional material, Shakespeare's plays can be seen in a romantic outdoor setting under the night sky at the Maynardville Open-Air Theater, Wynberg, during January and February. The Oude Libertas Arts Programme in Stellenbosch from January to March stages theatrical performances among the grapevines.

Live music can be heard at all the city's theaters. This ranges from classical to popular, and, increasingly, traditional and contemporary variations on African music. The Cape Town Philharmonic Orchestra plays at the Nico Theater most weeks, and this venue also stages lunchtime and Sunday afternoon concerts. The Cape Town Symphony Orchestra plays each week at City Hall.

Try to take in one of the summer outdoor performances at the Kirstenbosch National Botanical Gardens or the Josephine Mill at Newlands, and enjoy picnicking and listening to music in beautiful surroundings. Other venues include the South African Museum and the Agfa Amphitheater at the V&A

Waterfront, which regularly puts on free concerts.

Cape Town is renowned for its distinctive jazz, influenced by traditional African music, and made most famous by Abdullah Ibrahim (known as "Dollar Brand"). The Green Dolphin Restaurant (V&A Waterfront) and Dizzy's Jazz Café (Camps Bay) are two notable live jazz venues, while Mannenberg's

Local artists and street entertainers give the V&A Waterfront its unique vibe.

Jazz Café on Adderley and Church streets often sees terrific performances of Cape township jazz.

Nightclubs and Cinemas

Nightclubs tend to come and go in Cape Town. Many open at the start of the holiday season, but don't last once the tourists depart. The V&A Waterfront, and Loop and Long streets are the main pub and clubbing areas.

Cinemas are a very popular form of entertainment in and around Cape Town, and most of the major shopping malls have multi-screen complexes. The main cinemas are operated by Ster-Kinekor or Nu Metro, and tend to show the big Hollywood productions. Art cinemas include the Labia on Orange Street and the Baxter in Rondebosch, and the IMAX Cinema at the V&A Waterfront presents marvelous nature documentaries on one of the largest screens in the world.

> Tipping in restaurants isn't just a courtesy or tradition. Many waiters and waitresses are paid pitifully low wages, and depend on their tips for survival.

Art Galleries

Art lovers will find much to entertain them in Cape Town. The galleries and museums offer widely ranging exhibitions, covering everything from mysterious ancient rock paintings to European Old Masters to contemporary African art, sculpture and multimedia work.

An excellent Arts and Crafts map for the Western Cape is available free-of-charge through the tourism offices, and this details galleries, studios, and museums both in the city center and further afield.

The daily and weekly newspapers contain events listings which give guides to what's on, and it is definitely worth watch-

ing out for performances at unusual venues. Local radio station Good Hope FM is another good source of information, as is the web site (<www.mg.co.za>) which gives up-to-the-minute reports on fine art, music, movies, and theater in Cape Town and other key South African cities.

SPORTS

Capetonians, like all South Africans, are mad about sports, both watching them and taking part. The country's rugby and cricket teams are among the best in the world, and the national soccer team one of the best on the African continent. Cape Town's moderate climate means that many activities can be enjoyed year round. The geography of the region is perfect for all kinds of outdoor pursuits, including swimming, watersports, fishing, horse-riding, cycling, golf, and hiking.

This life cast of a San woman is one of many on display at the South African Museum.

Spectator Sports

Norwich Park, Newlands, is home to both the Western Province Rugby Football Union and the Western Province Cricket Association, and international and top-class national matches are played here. Details of forthcoming fixtures can be found in the local press.

Horse-racing is another very popular spectator sport. There are three race tracks, at Durbanville, Kenilworth, and Milnerton, and race horses are bred at Robertson. The J&B Metropolitan Handicap, held each year at Kenilworth, is a highly prestigious sporting and social event, where the fashions worn by race-goers are almost as important as what's happening on the track.

Every March, Cape Town plays host to the famous Argus Pick 'n Pay Cycle Tour. Over 30,000 competitors, including many from overseas, race along a stunning 105-km (65-mile) route around the Cape Peninsula. The sheer number of riders, plus the lavish costumes some wear, makes this a spectacular event to watch.

The city forms part of the route for many running marathons, the most important being the Cape Peninsula Marathon (February) and the 56-km- (35-mile-) long Two Oceans Marathon (April), both of which draw thousands of competitors.

Cape Town is a popular stopping-point for round-the-world yacht races, and every two years, the Cape to Rio Yacht Race leaves from here, with the next due to take place in January 2002. The Rothmans Week Sailing Regatta is held in Table Bay in December.

If You're Feeling Active

Sports enthusiasts are spoiled for choice in Cape Town. Huge amounts of money have been invested in sporting facilities which are, almost without exception, excellent.

If you're keen on golf you'll be in paradise, with 17 superb courses in glorious locations to choose from, including The Royal Cape at Wynberg, the country's oldest golf club, established in 1885. Most clubs welcome visitors on weekdays.

Horse-riding is another popular activity, and there are plenty of beautiful places to ride, including some beaches and vineyards. Mountain biking offers another form of mounted trans-

If you're looking for a break from the loads of touristy spots, escape to the pastoral beauty of Goukamma beach.

port. If you prefer to take your exercise on your own two feet, there are innumerable hiking trails throughout the national parks and reserves, and many hikers head for Table Mountain at weekends.

With so much coastline, it is not surprising that water-sport-lovers are well catered to. Some of the best surfers in the world make their home in Cape Town, and there are surfing competitions at Kommetjie, while windsurfing is rapidly growing in popularity. Scuba diving among the shipwrecks and kelp forests is a fascinating way to study the ecosystem off the Cape. Not all the beaches are suitable for swimming, either because of treacherous currents and pounding surf or because the water is simply too cold, but there are plenty of places where it is safe to swim (see page 92).

The same combination of the warm Indian Ocean and cooler Atlantic that makes the waters so alluring to divers is responsible for the remarkable wealth of marine life that brings fishermen in their droves. Standing, fishing rod in hand, on a virtually deserted beach, with golden-white sand stretching as far as the eye can see, is an idyllic experience few forget. Deep-sea game fishermen can charter boats to seek out swordfish, marlin, and yellow-fin tuna.

Those with a sense of adventure can enjoy white-water rafting along the Breede or Berg rivers, leap off Lion's Head and paraglide over Cape Town, or go shark-cage diving off Dyer Island. If a more serene form of outdoor activity appeals, hot-air ballooning over the winelands is probably the answer.

CHILDREN

Like all of South Africa, Cape Town is generally very welcoming to children, and there's plenty to keep the kids entertained.

The beaches are a huge family attraction, and most children are thrilled by the ride to the top of Table Mountain and the chance to spot baboons at the summit. Older children who really want to take on board some of the history of South Africa should find a trip to Robben Island thought-provoking and moving.

Many of the museums and exhibitions are geared to entertain younger visitors, notably the South African Museum, with its hands-on Discovery Room and fascinating Whale Well. The adjoining Planetarium offers regular children's shows. In Rosebank in the Southern Suburbs, the Baxter Theater has a very good children's theater.

The V&A Waterfront alone can keep children amused for days. The Telkom Exploratorium gives them a chance to learn about the history of telecommunication in a lively fashion. The floating exhibits at the South African National Maritime Museum are great to explore, and they can literally get to grips with life under the sea in the touch tanks of the Two Oceans Aquarium, or check out the sharks' diet at feeding time. The Aquarium also runs regular "sleepover"

Scenic Train Journeys

A train journey provides an unusual way to see the Cape. If time is short, have lunch on board Biggsy's Restaurant Carriage and Wine Bar as it runs from Cape Town to Simon's Town, passing some fine scenery along the False Bay Coast; Tel. (021) 449 3870.

If you have a day to spare, opt for the Outeniqua Choo Tjoe, the little steam train which runs through a glorious part of the Garden Route between Knysna and George (Tel. 044/801 8288). Alternatively, take a trip to the winelands on one of the classic engines of the Spier Vintage Train Company (Tel. 021/419 5222), or visit the Franschhoek Valley by steam train with Union Limited (Tel. 021/449 4391). Rovos Rail operates regular journeys between Cape Town and Knysna in 1940s carriages (Tel. 021/323 6052).

If budget and time are no problem, treat yourself to Union Limited's Golden Thread Tour, a six-day round-trip from Cape Town through the winelands, the Garden Route, Klein Karoo, and Oudtshoorn. Leaving the best for last, there's the legendary Blue Train, one of the most luxurious trains in the world, which runs between Cape Town and Pretoria (Tel. 011/773 7631), and the epic journeys operated by Shongolo Express (Tel. 011/453 3821). This latter combines cross-country rail travel by night with daytime excursions by minibuses, carried on board the train, in a 4,500-km (2,800-mile) trip from Cape Town to Johannesburg, via 24 of the 25 leading tourist destinations in South Africa.

If all this whets your appetite for vintage trains, check out the Outeniqua Railway Museum in George, or visit the Vorbaai Locomotive Yard in Hartenbos, both along the Garden Route. The latter is the biggest steam engine restoration center in South Africa, and attracts enthusiasts from around the world.

nights for children aged between seven and twelve. A ride on the Penny Ferry and a glimpse of the Cape fur seals is always entertaining, and the Waterfront's 300 shops provide the fastest way for kids to spend their holiday money. Other attractions here include the Scratch Patch on Dock Road, where they can scrabble for semi-precious stones, and the Indoor Grand Prix, where budding World Champions can try their hand at karting.

The jackass penguins at Boulder's Beach near Simon's Town, the gray squirrels in the Company's Gardens, and the sure-footed Swiss goats who live in the loft tower at the Fairview wine estate at Paarl will certainly be popular with the children, and even the most blasé teenager can't help but be impressed by the majestic sight of whales off the coast at Hermanus.

Children suffering withdrawal symptoms from theme parks will enjoy Ratanga Junction, at Century City. South Africa's first major theme park, it offers entertainment for

the whole family. Rides include the huge, bright-yellow Cobra rollercoaster and Crocodile Gorge. There are gentler rides for the tinies, plus "jungle cruises."

A word of warning if you are traveling with children under 12: some hotels do not accept them, so check before booking.

The Robberg Peninsula hosts teems of local wildlife like these tanning seals.

BEACHES

Cape Town's coastal suburbs boast unrivaled beaches, with great stretches of clean, golden sand, some literally miles long, with the ocean on one side, and majestic mountains on the other. Whether your preference is for quiet sheltered coves or wild open expanses of unspoiled dunes, for dozing in the sunshine, riding horses through the spray, or tackling long breaking waves on a surfboard, you'll find a beach close to Cape Town to suit you.

The beaches on the rugged Atlantic coast, which runs down the western side of the Cape Peninsula, while perfect for walking and sunbathing, aren't ideal for swimming, unless you're very hardy. The water temperature is chilly, seldom rising above 15°C, even in high summer. Those on the False Bay seaboard, north and east from Cape Point, benefit from warmer waters, though some have suffered from over-development. The wind off the ocean can be a problem all around the coast, whipping up the fine sand into a stinging cloud, and the beaches of False Bay are battered in the summer by vicious southeasterly winds.

On the Atlantic coast, the closest beaches to the city center are at Sea Point, but the sea is unsuitable for swimming here and the area generally unattractive. A little further south is the very fashionable resort of Clifton, with its anchorage of expensive yachts. It has four small beaches, all sandy, sheltered, and extremely popular with the young and beautiful. Swimming is safe, but the water painfully cold. Parking is a nightmare (don't even try in the peak summer season), but there are regular buses from the city center.

Camps Bay, a mile or so further south from Clifton, is another fashionable residential suburb, with fantastic views of Lion's Head, the Twelve Apostles mountains and the

Atlantic Ocean. The broad beach attracts families, and the town has many lively and affordable restaurants and cafés.

The stunning beach at Llandudno, 20 km (12 miles) south of Cape Town is a fabulous, sheltered cove set at the foot of a mountain, with giant boulders dominating the landscape. Sunsets are memorable, sunbathing idyllic and the surf highly dangerous. A twenty-minute walk from Llandudno is Sandy Bay, the main nudist beach for Cape Town. Accessible only by walking, it is an exceptionally pretty spot, with wildflowers and sand dunes, though nude sunbathing can be a painful experience when the wind off the ocean blows the sand around in great clouds!

Noordhoek, at the end of the thrilling journey along Chapman's Peak Drive, is incredibly impressive, with smooth white sand stretching for over 6 km (3.7 miles). Swimming can

Cherish the plush white sands of Noordhoek Beach — a perfect place for a reflective stroll or romantic interlude.

be hazardous off this gloriously wild beach, which is very popular with horse-riders, but walking along its vast shoreline is a relaxing experience to be cherished.

The water in the small basin at Kommetjie, a 15-km (9-mile) drive from Noordhoek, is wonderful for swimming, the temperature here a little higher than in the ocean. Surfers tackle the breakers at Long Beach, the site of serious surfing competitions.

The beaches within the Cape of Good Hope Nature Reserve are great for windswept walks and picnics, but few are suitable for swimming, though some have safe tidal pools.

Swimming is safe in the cove at Smitswinkelbaai on the False Bay coast, but the beach is accessible only by walking down a vast number of steps. Miller's Point has several sandy beaches and rare wildlife, including black zonure lizards, but 5 km (3 miles) north lies one of the most popular areas on the False Bay seaboard, Boulders. As the name implies, this series of small beaches is distinguished by numerous massive rocks, but its real claim to fame is the community of endangered jackass penguins who live here in a protected reserve on the beach. The combination of beautiful beach, crystal-clear rock pools, warm water and the sight of these wonderful black-and-white-birds, who love to mingle with the bathers, is irresistible to tens of thousands of tourists every year.

Fish Hoek has a superb family beach, with safe swimming and good facilities, while Muizenberg, northeast of Fish Hoek on the M4, and some 25 km (15 miles) from Cape Town, is overcrowded and faded, but its beach is still immensely popular, and there are plenty of family seaside activities like miniature golf.

The most popular beaches generally all have parking lots, but in high season it can be virtually impossible to find space. Those along the False Bay seaboard are well served by trains from Cape Town, and at the busiest times this is also the quickest way to get there.

Calendar of Events

There are so many exciting activities happening in and around Cape Town throughout the year that it would be impossible to cover them all in this guide. Cape Town Tourism and the various regional tourist boards will have full listings (see page 124).

January Minstrel Carnival, Cape Town (January 1–2); Cape to Rio Yacht Race, Cape Town (every two years), J&B Metropolitan Handicap, Kenilworth; Spier Festival, Stellenbosch

February Dias Festival, Mossel Bay; Cape Peninsula Marathon; Community Chest Carnival, Maynardville

March Argus Pick 'n Pay Cycle Tour; Stellenbosch Wine Festival; Worcester Pumpkin Festival; Western Cape Yellow fin Challenge, Hout Bay; Nederburg Wine Auction, Paarl

April Two Oceans Marathon, Cape Town (Easter Sunday); Franschhoek Festival

May Whale-watching begins

June Snoek Festival, Hout Bay

July Bastille Festival, Franschhoek; Knysna Oyster Festival, Berg River Canoe Marathon, Paarl; Port Festival, Calitzdorp

August Calamari Festival, Plettenberg Bay; Lipton Cup Yacht Race, Cape Town; Hout Bay Festival

September Darling Art Festival; Darling Wild Flower and Orchid Show; Fernkloof Wild Flower Show, Hermanus; Whale Festival, Hermanus; Spring Flower Show, Kirstenbosch National Botanical Gardens; Stellenbosch Festival

October Food & Wine Festival, Stellenbosch; Oudtshoorn Ostrich Festival; Spring Regatta, Table Bay

November Fireworks Festival, Saldanha; The Winelands Marathon, Stellenbosch

December Christmas Carols, Greenmarket Square; Crayfish Festival, Lambert's Bay; Rothmans Week Sailing Regatta, Table Bay

EATING OUT

Even the choosiest eaters will find something to suit their appetite in Cape Town. The city is famed for the quality and range of its cuisine, and it is remarkably easy to eat out well without blowing the holiday budget.

Whether you want a tasty snack in an informal bistro or an elegant candlelit dinner in sumptuous surroundings, you'll find it in and around Cape Town. The V&A Waterfront alone is home to a vast range of eateries to suit all tastes and pockets, while the Southern Suburbs and Winelands towns — Franschhoek in particular — boast many fine restaurants, often in superb old Cape Dutch buildings. There are also restaurants in breathtaking locations, such as Bientang's Cave, in a cave overlooking the ocean at Hermanus. Sidewalk cafés have increased in numbers in Cape Town in recent years. Saturday morning breakfast outside Mozart's Café near Greenmarket Square, serenaded by buskers, has become a Cape Town tradition.

> **If you don't specify that you want it plain, steak and seafood often comes smothered in spicy sauce.**

As befits a cosmopolitan city, the cuisine of many countries is well represented, including Chinese, French, Greek, Italian, Indian, Japanese, Thai, and Turkish, and, of course, pizza and the ubiquitous hamburger are readily available. In addition, restaurants offering traditional food from other parts of Africa are on the increase.

With the Mediterranean climate and so many beautiful beaches and glorious countryside so close at hand, it is not surprising that picnics are popular. Many beaches have dedicated picnic areas, and excellent, easily portable food, including huge "submarine" sandwiches, can be brought from delicatessens. Some hotels will prepare picnics for their guests to take with them, and the vineyards will often sell filled picnic baskets, to be enjoyed in their leafy grounds.

What to Eat

Cape Malay Cuisine

The city's history can be traced through its food. Dutch, English, French, German and Portuguese culinary influences have all played a part, but the most significant is that of the "Malay" slaves who came from the East Indies in the 17th century.

Local Cape Malay specialities include *bobotie*, a sweet-ish curried minced lamb served with savory custard; *sosaties*, a sort of marinated kebab; *bredie*, a spicy stew traditionally made from venison or mutton, and often accompanied by a sweetened vegetable or fruit dish, and *smoorsnoek,* lightly-curried snoek, a local linefish.

Restaurants specializing in this cuisine are few and far between, but include Cape Manna on Napier Street. However, Cape Malay dishes can be found on the wider menus of many restaurants, so it is not difficult to sample this local fare. For the ultimate treat, head for Cape Colony in the Mount Nelson Hotel.

Stunning Seafood

For a city so close to the ocean, really excellent seafood is unexpectedly hard to find in Cape Town itself, though Ocean

Visit Die Strandloper on Langebaan beach if you're a big fan of barbecue.

Basket is a very popular seafood bistro chain, offering good, inexpensive food in friendly, unpretentious surroundings.

Once you head towards the shores, the choice, freshness and quality is simply outstanding. Shellfish, including crayfish, lobsters, oysters (often served with hot chilli sauce), and mussels are in plentiful supply, as are the extremely tasty linefish, including snoek, yellowtail, kinglip, kabeljou and geelbek. Since the Russians decimated the Mozambique prawn beds with over-fishing, prawns have tended to be expensive.

South Africans love to *braai* — barbecue — and seafood lends itself particularly well to this form of cooking. If you're fond of fish, try to make the time to head along the coastal roads to of one of the open-air seafood restaurants, especially Die Strandloper on the beach at Langebaan. Here you get the chance, over a 10-course meal, to taste the freshest-imaginable seafood the Western Cape has to offer.

Meat, Meat... and More Meat

Most South Africans are great meat eaters, and the range of meat and poultry on offer is impressive. Beef, pork, chicken, and mutton are often joined on the menu by more exotic varieties, including ostrich and crocodile.

Steak remains one of the most common choices, often accompanied by monkey-gland sauce (a sort of chutney). French fries or baked potatoes are the usual accompaniments, together with a host of vegetables. Steakhouse chains such as Spurs are always popular, and are usually a good option for those with children, providing coloring books etc. to keep them entertained.

The influence of early German settlers can be seen in the great range of highly-spiced *boerewors* ("farmer's sausages") available.

Biltong, dried meat, is a South African speciality which evolved centuries ago when meat could best be preserved by spicing, salting, and drying. Beef biltong is the most common, but it is also made from game. It can be bought packaged in strips, and is increasingly to be found on restaurant menus, usually shaved over salad. Trying it is a must, but it is not to everyone's taste!

Breakfast Afrikaans-style is a hearty affair, often including many eggs, several rashers of bacon, plus steak. Don't panic if you can't face such huge feasts, it is equally easy to start the day with muffins or fresh fruit.

Vegetarians needn't despair. A huge selection of fresh salads and vegetables are available all year round, with most menus offering vegetarian options. There are also specialist vegetarian restaurants.

Desserts

Desserts are often delicious but all-too-frequently laden with calories. Local delicacies include *malva*, made from cream, sugar and apricot conserve, and Cape brandy pudding, a steamed pudding soaked with brandy. Equally tasty, but less guilt-inducing, are fresh fruit kebabs. If you don't have a sweet tooth, or if you still have room after dessert, South African cheeses are very good, and you'll usually be offered local versions of the European classics such as brie.

What to Drink

What else, in the shadow of Table Mountain, but Cape wine? Local labels are served almost everywhere, and the choice and price range excellent. South African white wines are admired around the world, but the reds are quite superb. Pinotage, which was developed in Stellenbosch, should definitely be tried.

Not all restaurants have alcohol licenses, but the Cape is so steeped in wine culture that it is common practice to bring your own wine, even to the most upmarket eatery, and corkage is usually either not charged, or very low.

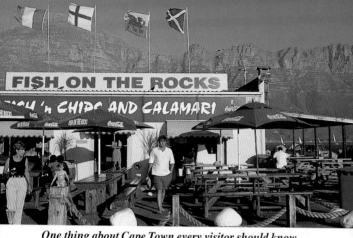

*One thing about Cape Town every visitor should know...
There's never a shortage of great places to eat!*

Lager is also a popular choice, usually served very cold, and microbreweries are now emerging, including Mitchells at the V&A Waterfront. For non-drinkers, there's a vast choice of fresh fruit juices, including apricot, guava, and pear, plus the usual soft drinks.

When to Eat

Breakfast is available from coffee shops from about 9am (though in the city center many open earlier), and lingering over a hearty breakfast while watching the world go by is a good start to a day's sightseeing. Afternoon tea is served at certain hotels and coffee shops, while most restaurants offer both lunch and dinner, with dinner generally served from 6:30pm until about 10pm, though in areas such as the V&A Waterfront they may be open later.

It is worth checking the opening times in advance, to avoid disappointment. Also remember not all restaurants are open every day. The most popular can sometimes be fully-booked for weeks in advance, so securing a table can be a problem if you're on a short holiday, unless you book before you travel.

Restaurant Etiquette

Formal restaurants may not welcome children, and may forbid entry to anyone wearing jeans or shorts, though informal dress isn't a problem elsewhere. Restaurants have to offer a non-smoking section.

Rooibos Tea

Don't leave Cape Town without trying one of the indigenous specialities — rooibos tea.

This remarkably versatile product was first discovered over a hundred years ago, by the Coloured population of the Cederberg area. They picked the wild *Aspalanthus linearis*, known as rooibos ("red bush"), and bruised the leaves with hammers before drying them in the sun and making a refreshing, tea-like drink.

In 1905 a Russian immigrant, Benjamin Ginsberg, began to exploit its potential, and by the 1930s the town of Clanwilliam had become the center for rooibos tea production. Today it is available as loose tea or tea bags, is drunk throughout South Africa, and exported around the world.

It is low in tannin and free of additives and caffeine, so very good for you. It is alleged to help those suffering from insomnia, indigestion, hay fever, and even nappy diaper rash (applied, cold, to the skin in this last case!), while house plants are said to thrive on regular waterings with cold rooibos tea. It can also be used for cooking, incorporated into soups, cakes, stews, and all manner of hot and cold drinks.

Visitors to Clanwilliam, an elegant old town in the shadows of the Cederberg mountains, can tour the vast fields of rooibos, and see the processing sheds. Rooibos tea recipes can be found on the Internet at <www.rooibosltd.co.za>.

HANDY TRAVEL TIPS

An A–Z Summary of Practical Information

A

ACCOMMODATIONS (see also Recommended Hotels on pages 127–134)

Cape Town and its environs offer a wide range of accommodations of all standards and prices, from the simplest backpackers' hostels and charming self-catering cottages to 5-star luxury hotels on a par with the best in the world.

Bear in mind that accommodation is in tremendous demand during the peak season (November–April), and particularly during the South African school summer holidays (early-December to mid-January), when prices can rise by up to 50%. Advance booking is essential during these times. Cape Town Tourism (Tel. 021/418 5214) will help with bookings and advice on all types of accommodation. The national tourist authority, SATOUR, issues an annual, nationwide accommodation listing, in which it divides hotels into five categories denoted by one to five stars, with a five-star rating marking the most luxurious establishments. (Tel. 012/347 0600.)

Hotel chains including Holiday Inn and Protea offer good, if uninspiring, accommodation. For the same (or often less) money, you can usually find smaller, independent hotels, which are full of character. Throughout the Western Cape you will encounter these extremely well-run establishments, often in quiet locations with beautiful gardens. The area is also particularly well-endowed with fine guest houses and B&Bs. Many are in elegant, old gabled Cape Dutch houses, and offer excellent value. The Guest House Association of Southern Africa supplies information on this form of accommodation (Tel. 021/762 4912). In addition, self-catering cottages, often in stunning locations, are available to rent by the sea or on farms.

The V&A Waterfront area is an enjoyable place to stay in the city center. The main hotels here are set slightly away from the busy nightlife spots, so it is not too noisy, and many of the restaurants are open later than others in Cape Town. The historic city center is virtually deserted at night; arguably uncomfortably so, while the southern suburbs are an excellent source of quiet, comfortable hotels in safe areas within easy striking distance of the city center's attractions.

Mid to lower-priced hotels will usually offer family rooms, but many of the expensive hotels in Cape Town and around the Western Cape often won't accept children aged under 12. This is unfortunate, as many of these are set in the most fascinating parts of the Cape.

AIRPORT

Cape Town's International Airport is 22 km (13 miles) east of the city center. It has international and domestic terminals, a bureau de change, duty-free facilities, car rental offices, hotel booking kiosks, information desks, taxis, and a VAT refund office. There are no trains from the airport, but shuttle buses operate to and from the city center and main hotels (airport shuttle: Tel. 021/386 4414), and a taxi fare to the city will cost in the region of R120. Flight information: Tel. (021) 934 0407.

B

BUDGETING FOR YOUR TRIP

Favorable exchange rates mean that it is easy to enjoy a high standard of accommodation and catering in Cape Town without spending a fortune. To most visitors from the US it will seem inexpensive, and European visitors will consider it a positive bargain.

The prices below should give you an indication of how much you will be charged:

Airfares

These vary hugely, according to the time of year and which class you choose to fly. April and May are usually the cheapest times to fly, and December and January the most expensive. Round-trip flights from the US can cost in the region of $1,200–$2,200 (low season– high season), from the UK or Europe about £600–£1000, and from Australia A$1750–A$2000. Package tours are available, which reduce the costs significantly.

Accommodations
A double room in a luxurious five-star hotel will cost anywhere from R600–R1500 per night; in a good three-star hotel upwards of R300 per night, and about R200 in a B&B. Apart from the most expensive establishments, breakfast is generally included in the price of your room.

Meals and Drinks
Although prices will vary dramatically according to the restaurant chosen, an average three-course meal will cost R50–R150, a bottle of wine in a restaurant R30–R50 and a cup of tea or coffee R4–R6.

Sightseeing
Many of the museums and galleries offer either free admission or charge only a nominal entry fee.

Taxis
A trip in one of the tourist-friendly Rikkis should cost between R5 and R15. Metered taxis charge about R5 per kilometer.

CAMPING
Camping is enormously popular in South Africa, with a good net-work of campsites in the rural areas and national parks around Cape Town. Private resorts are much better than the municipal campsites, in terms of washing and cooking facilities and safety, while rough camping isn't recommended under any circumstances; it simply isn't safe. Private resorts will often offer self-catering accommodation, shops, cafés or restaurants, barbecue stands, and a swimming pool.

Cape Town

CAR RENTAL/HIRE (see also DRIVING)

Though public transport in Cape Town is amongst the best in South Africa, the story isn't always the same outside the city. With so many magnificent destinations to travel to, a car is invaluable.

Cars can be rented from desks at the airport and the rental companies' own offices in the city. There are many in Cape Town, including Avis (Tel. 0800 021111), Budget (Tel. 0800 016622), Europcar (Tel. 0800 011344), and Hertz (Tel. 0800 600136). Leading South African firms include Imperial (Tel. 0800 131000) and Tempest (Tel. 0800 031666). Classic Twin Tours hire out Harley-Davidson motor cycles and classic MG sports cars; Tel. (021) 882 2558.

Car rental isn't inexpensive here, but rivalry between the big international names and smaller local organizations ensures that there are good deals to be had if you shop around. Local firms are generally cheaper, but if you decide to rent a car through one of the international names, you can pick it up in one city and deposit it in another.

Check that the rental includes collision damage and theft waivers, and breakdown and accident rescue, and also be aware that some insurance doesn't extend to motoring on dirt roads. With so much to see around Cape Town, unlimited mileage is a more than sensible option. Some companies offer very good deals which include a mobile phone on which one can make and receive international calls, with no charge for incoming calls.

If your own driving license isn't printed in English and doesn't bear your photograph, you will need an International Driving Permit to rent a car, which you must obtain before you arrive in South Africa. Most companies insist on the driver being aged at least 21, with some stipulating a minimum age of 23 or even 25.

Motor home rental is also big business in Cape Town. It is a great way to travel to remote places, and with the excellent campsites in national parks, there are plenty of attractive destinations to head for.

Although you'll save on accommodation, it is not a cheap option. Rental is usually fairly high, as is gasoline (petrol) consumption. Most gas stations only take cash for fuel, so you may have to carry more cash to remote areas than you are comfortable with. Big motor home rental companies with offices in Cape Town include Britz Africa (Tel. 021/981 8947), and Rainbow Camper Hire (Tel. 021/948 0743). Knysna Camper Hire (Tel. 0445/ 22444) is a good rental company along the Garden Route.

CLIMATE

South Africa's climate is the reverse of that of the northern hemisphere, with mid-winter in June and July and high summer in December and January. It is always a few degrees cooler by the coast than inland. Cape Town has a Mediterranean climate, with cool, wet winters and warm to hot, dry summers. Autumn (March–May) and Spring (September–November) are the wettest seasons, with short periods of heavy rain. Though the climate is temperate, it is liable to change suddenly, switching from bright sunshine to gray skies within minutes.

The chart below gives Cape Town's average minimum and maximum temperatures.

	J	F	M	A	M	J	J	A	S	O	N	D
Max °C	26	27	26	23	20	18	17	18	19	21	24	25
Max °F	79	80	79	74	68	64	63	64	66	70	75	77
Min °C	16	16	15	13	11	9	8	9	10	12	14	15
Min °F	61	61	59	55	52	48	46	48	50	54	57	59

Weather Forecast: Tel. (021) 934 0450/8.

CLOTHING

Informal clothing (e.g., shorts and T-shirt) is generally accepted everywhere, though most restaurants prefer smart casual dress, and some require men to wear a jacket and tie, particularly after 6pm. Always be prepared for the weather to change. Even in high summer it is advisable to take a jacket or sweater with you for sudden drops in temperature, or to wear on boat trips. Remember to pack sensible shoes, which will be invaluable for lengthy sightseeing walks, or hikes through forests or National Parks.

CRIME AND SAFETY

The usual rules of self-preservation which apply in any major city should be followed with extra vigilance in Cape Town. The golden rule is to be sensible and be aware of what's happening around you.

Don't walk alone after dark, and don't be ostentatious; never display expensive jewelry or cameras when walking around. If you think you're being followed, change direction or vary the pace you walk at. When returning to your hotel after dark, always use the main entrance, and avoid unlit places.

Use credit cards and travelers' checks, and keep the amount of cash you carry to a minimum. Watch out for groups of small children surrounding you, and don't carry valuables in easily-accessible pockets. Remember, pick-pockets and muggers will pick the easiest targets; they don't want to get caught! If the worst happens and you are mugged, remain calm and don't resist, as guns are all too common.

When traveling by car, be aware that car-jacking is on the increase in Cape Town. Again, there are obvious precautions to take: keep doors locked and shut all windows whenever the car has to stop; plan your route in advance and make long journeys during daylight only; store personal items out of sight; park only in well-lit areas, and never pick up hitchhikers.

Never venture into the Cape Flats townships unless on a guided tour. Remember, however, that in spite of the horror stories, most crime is centered on areas tourists seldom visit, while areas such as the Garden Route and Little Karoo are extremely safe. If you follow these basic, sensible precautions there is no need to be paranoid about crime in the Cape, and you can relax and enjoy this wonderful place.

CUSTOMS AND ENTRY REQUIREMENTS

All visitors to South Africa need a passport valid for at least six months. Citizens of the US, EU, Australia, Canada, and New Zealand currently don't need a visa. As regulations are subject to change, it is a good idea to check with your travel agent.

You will need a valid return ticket, or you must be able to show that you have the funds to buy one, and, if asked, you must be able to prove that you can support yourself while in the country.

Duty-Free Allowance

Travelers aged 18 and over are allowed to bring in 400 cigarettes, 250 grams of tobacco and 50 cigars, one liter of spirits, two liters of wine, 50 ml of perfume and 250 ml of toilet water, plus gifts and other souvenirs up to the value of R500. No person under 18 is entitled to the alcohol or tobacco allowance. Duty is levied at 20% over these allowances.

VAT is charged at 14%. However, foreign tourists can reclaim the VAT they pay on goods (but not on services) with a total value of more than R250. The VAT Refund Office is based at Cape Town International Airport. You'll need your passport and the original invoice and may have to fill out a reclamation form (available at the Refund Office at the Airport and also in Victoria Wharf at the V&A Waterfront). You must reclaim VAT before you check in your luggage, if you have already packed the relevant items. If you can't produce the goods, if asked, the money won't be refunded. There is an administration charge equivalent to 2% of the VAT paid, and refunds can be made in any currency.

Currency

There is no limit to the amount of foreign currency or travelers' checks you can import, but importing and exporting Rand is limited to R500 in notes, so if you have more than R500 in cash at the end of your trip, be sure to reconvert before you leave the country.

D

DRIVING (see also CRIME AND SAFETY)

Road Conditions

With its excellent network of roads and light traffic, driving in South Africa can be very enjoyable. The road surfaces are generally good, with wide hard shoulders. However, these same conditions also encourage recklessness, and the country has an unenviable accident record, with drunken driving and badly loaded, unstable vehicles among the prime causes.

Apart from drunken and/or speeding drivers, another hazard on the road to watch out for is animals, particularly at night in country areas, so heed the warning signs.

Minibus taxis in the Cape have an unwritten right of way, and they also frequently run red lights. Their drivers often carry handguns, so it is not a good idea to object to their driving if you encounter one on the road.

You may find overtaking drivers coming towards you, who will assume that you will move over to the hard shoulder to avoid an accident.

Rules and Regulations

Foreign drivers' licenses, printed in English, and bearing the driver's photograph are valid in South Africa for up to six months. Drivers not in possession of a license meeting these criteria must obtain an International Driving Permit before they travel. You must have your driver's license with you at all times while driving.

South Africans drive on the left hand side of the road, and speed limits are 60 km/h (37 mph) in built-up areas, 100 km/h (60 mph) on country roads and 120 km/h (73 mph) on major highways. Though there are heavy fines for those caught exceeding these limits, Capetonians frequently do so.

There are few roundabouts, but you may encounter four-way stops. The rule here is that the person who gets to a stop sign first has right of way over drivers arriving at the other stops. At roundabouts and other junctions, give way to traffic coming from the right. Be aware that Capetonians tend to run red lights.

You are compelled by law to wear a seat belt.

Fuel Costs

Compared to European prices, fuel is cheap in Cape Town, though it costs a little more to fill up here than it does in the US. There are plenty of filling stations on the main roads, but far less when you venture off the beaten track. In the city center many will be open 24 hours, and from 7am–7pm in other urban areas. Opening hours can be much shorter in rural areas, so be sure to fill up when you get the opportunity. In most cases only cash is accepted to pay for fuel.

Parking

There are a good number of car parks in Cape Town, and lots of parking meters. You'll also see many self-proclaimed "parking attendants," who will, in return for a small payment, guide you to a parking space, then guard your car while you're away. If you're not happy with this idea, don't be intimidated; you're not compelled to park where they say. If you do decide to make use of their services, however, insist on paying when you return to your car, as you have no guarantees that they'll stay with your car if you pay in advance.

It is illegal to park on the opposite side of the road facing the oncoming traffic.

If You Need Help

If you're involved in an accident in which no one is injured, you must inform the police within 24 hours. If someone is hurt, you mustn't move the vehicles involved until the police have arrived. Give your name and insurance details to the driver of the other vehicle involved, and get theirs.

Cape Town

If your car breaks down, pull in to the left and put a red warning triangle 50 m (about 160 ft) behind the car. The Automobile Association of South Africa can be called upon for advice and emergency rescue (Tel. 0800 010101), and may have a reciprocal arrangement with a driving association in your own country.

Road Signs

Road signs are generally in both English and Afrikaans. Occasionally they will only be in Afrikaans, so make sure you know the name of your destination in that language. For example, Cape Town is Kaapstad. When traveling on dirt roads, be aware that it is easy to become slightly disoriented, and think you've traveled farther than you have. If you're expecting a destination to be signed, wait until you see that sign until you turn off. Don't head off on any unsigned roads you may reach before.

Fluid measures

Distance

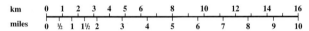

ELECTRICITY

The power supply is 220/240 volts at 50 cycles per second (Hz). Most hotels have 110 volt sockets for electric razors. Take a three-point, round-pinned adapter for hairdryers, etc., though they're readily available to buy if you forget.

EMBASSIES/CONSULATES/HIGH COMMISSIONS

Most embassies are in Johannesburg, but many countries have consulates in Cape Town.

Australia (High Commission): 14th Floor, No. 1 Thibault Square; Tel. (021) 419 5425.

Canada (High Commission): 19th Floor, 60 SA reserve Bank, corner of George and Hout streets; Tel. (021) 423 5240.

Ireland: no representative in Cape Town; call the High Commission in Johannesburg for assistance; Tel. (011) 836 5869.

UK (consulate): 15th Floor, Southern Life Building, 8 Riebeeck Street; Tel. (021) 425 3670.

US (consulate): 7th Floor, Monte Carlo Building, Herengracht Street; Tel. (021) 421 4280.

New Zealand: no representative in Cape Town; call the High Commission in Pretoria for assistance; Tel. (012) 342 8656.

EMERGENCIES

Ambulance: Tel. 101777

Police Flying Squad: Tel. 10111

Fire Brigade: Tel. (021) 535 1100

GAY AND LESBIAN TRAVELERS

Cape Town welcomes gay and lesbian travelers. South Africa has a progressive, gay- and lesbian-friendly constitution, and the city is the gay capital of the country. There are many gay clubs and restaurants, and an annual drag ball, held in December or January. Useful information is available through the Pink Guide (available from tourist offices) and Gay Net (Tel. 021/422 1925; web site <www.gaynetcapetown.co.za>). Bear in mind that open displays of affection between gay couples are less tolerated in rural areas.

Cape Town

GETTING THERE

By Air

There are an increasing number of direct flights to Cape Town International Airport from major European and US cities, including London, Atlanta, and New York. The majority of travelers from Europe and North America used to fly via Johannesburg, though this is now changing rapidly.

High season (September–March, but especially December and January) is the most expensive time to travel, while winter and spring (April–October) is the cheapest.

Many tour operators offer package tours from North America, Europe or the UK. These tours can be all-inclusive, covering everything from flights, accommodation, car hire or local transport, meals, and excursions to areas such as the Garden Route and winelands. They can represent significant savings on booking all elements individually, though you may find yourself tied in to a group itinerary. Companies such as Union-Castle Travel in London, England (Tel. +44 207 229 1411) will tailor-make holidays for individuals with a less restricted budget, preparing itineraries to suit the specific interests of their clients.

Fly-Drive deals are also available through many airlines in conjunction with the international car rental companies.

Transport from Cape Town International Airport to the city center is by taxi or shuttle bus.

By Rail

Trains operate daily to Cape Town from other parts of South Africa, covering vast distances in journeys which can last up to 24 hours. A popular, if expensive, option with some tourists is to travel to Cape Town from elsewhere in South Africa on one of the famous luxury trains which offer an irresistible combination of lavish accommodation and glorious, ever-changing scenery. The best-known of these is the Blue Train, which journeys between Cape Town and Pretoria (see also page 90).

By Sea

As befits a destination with a such a long association with seafarers, Cape Town is on the route for a number of cruise lines, and it is also possible to travel as a passenger on board a cargo ship. The skyline has obviously changed dramatically since Bartolomeu Dias first ordered his ship steered in the direction of Table Mountain, but arriving by sea is still memorable.

GUIDES AND TOURS

Innumerable tour companies operate in the region, offering anything from a half-day tour of the V&A Waterfront or historic city center, to trips along the Garden Route or Western Coast lasting over a week. All tour guides speak English, and many will also speak French, German, or Spanish. Certain areas, such as the Cape Flats, should only be visited as part of a tour party, while only official tours are allowed to land on Robben Island.

Legend Tours (Tel. 021/697 4056) will take you around the Bo-Kaap, District Six, Cape Flats, and Robben Island. Flamingo Adventure Tours offer tours for disabled travelers and their companions to all major attractions (Tel. 021/557 4496; web site <www.time2travel.com/ct/flamingto/index>). The CapeVine arranges tours centered on wine, food, heritage, or wildlife (Tel. 021/913 6611).

HEALTH AND MEDICAL CARE

Cape Town has excellent medical services. Doctors are listed in the telephone directory under "Medical Practitioners," and hotels will usually call one for a guest, if required. Although patients are generally referred to a hospital by a doctor, in an emergency head straight for the casualty department of the nearest hospital. Outpatient treatment is available at relatively low cost, though you should take out medical insurance before you travel.

Cape Town

The biggest hospital in Cape Town is Groote Schuur (Hospital Drive, Observatory; Tel. 021/404 9111). The world's first heart transplant operation took place here, in 1967. City Park Hospital on the corner of Longmarket and Bree streets is convenient to the historic city center, and has a trauma surgeon available 24 hours a day (Tel. 0801 222 222 or 0802 234 835). Somerset Hospital on Beach Road, Mouille Point also has outpatient and emergency departments (Tel. 021/402 6911), and is convenient to the V&A Waterfront.

Pharmacies

Consult the Yellow Pages for the pharmacy closest to you. Not all pharmacies are open outside of regular shopping hours, but those with extended opening hours include: Hypermed Pharmacy, York Road and Main Road, Green Point; Tel. (021) 434 1414, open 8:30am–9pm Monday–Saturday, and 9am–9pm Sunday; K's Pharmacy, 52 Regent Road, Sea Point; Tel. (021) 434 9331, open 9am–9pm daily.

No inoculations are mandatory for travel to anywhere in South Africa. It is, however, advisable to make sure that your tetanus and polio vaccinations are current.

Stomach upsets are rare as tap water is safe to drink, and ice and salad in restaurants are also safe. The area isn't a malarial zone. The greatest hazard to tourists is the African sun. Skin cancer is on the increase, so using a strong sunscreen and wearing a sun hat are essential. It is easy to burn as there is often a gentle breeze, so the scorching sun can feel deceptively cool. Rabies is present in the area, so assume the worst if you're bitten by an animal and go to hospital for treatment.

HOLIDAYS

January 1	New Years Day
March 21	Human Rights Day
Good Friday	(moveable)

Easter Sunday	(moveable)
Family Day	(Easter Monday)
April 27	Freedom Day
May 1	Workers' Day
June 16	Youth Day
August 9	National Woman's Day
September 24	Heritage Day
December 16	Day of Reconciliation
December 25	Christmas Day
December 26	Day of Goodwill

L

LANGUAGE

There are 11 official languages in South Africa, with the three most common in the Western Cape being Afrikaans, English, and Xhosa. English is the language of administration, so almost everyone speaks it, at least to some degree.

If you want to try some Afrikaans, the following phrases and vocabulary will be useful:

Good morning	*Goeie môre*
Good afternoon	*Goeie middag*
Good night	*Goeie nag*
Goodbye	*Tot siens*
Please	*Asseblief*
Thank you	*Dankie*
How much...?	*Hoeveel...?*

Cape Town

What is the time?	*Hoe laat is dit?*		
Where is…?	*Waar is…?*		

Numbers:

one	een	six	ses
two	twee	seven	sewe
three	drie	eight	agt
four	vier	nine	nege
five	vyf	ten	tien

Afrikaans is very closely related to Dutch. The "g" is pronounced with a guttural "kh," "oe" is pronounced "oo," and "v" is pronounced "f."

M

MAPS

The excellent Cape Town Tourism, the national tourist authority SATOUR, and regional tourist offices provide very good maps, usually free of charge (see page 123 for contact information). In addition, maps are available at most book shops. You will need more detailed maps if you plan to head off the main routes and explore the dirt roads.

MEDIA

Radio And Television

There are three public television channels; SABC 1, 2, and 3. SABC 1 broadcasts almost entirely in English, and puts out a mix of soap operas, news, documentaries, game shows, and American imports, and the other two channels broadcast a mixture of several languages. The English-language satellite network is M-Net, and CNN is available when SABC isn't broadcasting. BBC World Service TV can also be found in some hotels.

The English-language SAFM radio station provides good morning and evening news programs, and the BBC World Service and Voice of America can be picked up on short-wave frequencies.

Newspapers

Newspapers are published in English and Afrikaans. National English-language newspapers include the *Sowetan* and *Star* (both daily), the *Sunday Times*, and the weekly *Mail & Guardian*. *Business Day* is a national financial daily, and there are two daily English-language local Cape Town newspapers, the *Cape Times* and *Cape Argus*. CNA newsagent shops sell many international publications including *Newsweek, Time*, the *Daily Mail* and *Daily Telegraph*.

MONEY

Currency

The South African currency, the Rand, is divided into 100 cents. R200, R100, R50, R20, and R10 bank notes are issued.

Exchange Facilities

Money can be changed at banks, bureaux de change, and branches of Rennies Travel (Thomas Cook) in St. George's Street (Tel. 021/25 2370) or at the V&A Waterfront (Tel. 021/418 3744). Some hotels also offer an exchange facility, but charge a high commission. Bureaux de change include Trustbank at Cape Town International Airport (Tel. 021/934 0223) and American Express at the V&A Waterfront (Tel. 021/419 3917).

Travelers' Checks And Credit Cards

Travelers' checks are accepted by many hotels, restaurants, and shops in the city. International credit cards including American Express, Diners Club, MasterCard, and Visa are also accepted, but rarely for gas (petrol).

ATMs

Automatic Teller Machines operate 24 hours a day outside most banks.

OPEN HOURS

Banks are open 9am–3:30pm Monday–Friday and 9am–11am Saturday, but bureaux de change are generally open at least until 5pm and sometimes later.

Most shops are typically open from 8:30am–5pm Monday–Friday, and until 1pm on Saturday. Although, supermarkets and many liquor stores tend to close later — around 6pm, Monday–Friday and 5pm on Saturday. In the city center, you will also find many shops open later, and some open on Sunday mornings. Many shops at the V&A Waterfront offer late-night shopping (most until 9pm) seven days a week.

POLICE

In an emergency contact the Police Flying Squad: Tel. 10111

Members of the South African Police are armed, and wear blue uniforms and peaked caps. The growing importance of tourism to South Africa is producing a police force which is more tourist-friendly, but their image is recovering from past associations as the enforcers of apartheid, and they are not respected by many citizens. Consequently, they may not appear over-enthusiastic about solving crime if you are robbed, but you will need to report incidents to them, and to produce some form of identification when you do so.

POST OFFICES

The main post office in Cape Town is on Parliament Street; Tel. (021) 461 5670. Its opening hours are 8am–4:30pm Monday, Tuesday, Thursday, and Friday, 8:30am–4:30pm Wednesday and 8am–12 noon on Saturday. Smaller post offices will be closed at lunchtime (1pm–2pm). Post offices handle mail, parcels, and telegrams. Mailboxes are painted red.

PUBLIC TRANSPORTATION

Unlike many other South African cities, Cape Town has reasonable public transport.

Buses

A good bus network operates between the city center and the V&A Waterfront, Table Mountain, the Southern Suburbs, Kirstenbosch National Botanical Gardens, and most popular beaches along the False Bay coast. Buy your ticket from the driver on entry. If you plan to travel by bus a great deal during your visit, a Ten Ride Clip Card can prove a sensible purchase.

A number of luxury intercity coach companies operate from Cape Town along the major tourist routes such as the Garden Route. These include Intercape Coaches (Tel. 021/419 8888).

Railway

Trains run very frequently at peak times from the city center through the suburbs to Simon's Town on the False Bay coast. The stations aren't signposted, so you'll need a map to help you find them. Tickets should be bought in advance from the station, and timetables can be bought at the station or from newsagents.

Taxis

There are three types of taxi available — Rikkis, metered taxis, and minibus taxis.

Rikkis are a highly tourist-friendly form of transport. You can hail these three-wheeled vehicles from the street or order one by phone (Tel. 021/423 4888). They take several passengers, but it is possible to hire one on an exclusive basis for short tours to destinations such as Cape Point.

Metered taxis are available from taxi ranks around the city, or can be ordered by phone. They're not the cheapest form of transport, but at night are definitely the safest alternative to driving yourself.

Minibus taxis aren't recommended for tourists. Unlike metered taxis, they can be hailed from the street, but are usually driven recklessly. They are often owned by rival factions, and the drivers generally carry guns.

R

RELIGION

Although the majority of South Africans are Christian, all denominations are represented, and Cape Town has many places of worship, including churches, mosques, temples, and synagogues. Hotels, tourist information offices, and local newspapers give details of where they can be found.

T

TELEPHONE/FAX/E-MAIL

The dialing code for Cape Town from overseas is +27, 21, and 021 from within South Africa. The international access code to dial out of South Africa is 09, followed by the relevant country code.

There are plenty of Telkom public phone booths in Cape Town, from which domestic and international calls may be made. The green public phones use telephone cards, available from post offices, the airport, bookshops, and certain supermarkets and hotels. The cards are available in amounts from R10 to R100. Public and private telephones offer direct dialing to countries around the world. International calls from South Africa are cheapest 8pm–8am Monday to Friday and Saturday afternoon through Sunday night.

The directory enquiry service is free, and can be accessed by calling 1023 (domestic numbers) or 0903 (international numbers). Bear in mind that the operator may not speak English as their main language, so be prepared to talk slowly and clearly, repeating yourself if necessary.

Cellular telephones, operating on the GSM digital system, work well and are extremely common. Travelers bringing their own mobile phones with them should check the roaming agreement with their service provider. A cheaper option is to rent a phone once you arrive. Visit the Vodacom rental desk at Cape Town International Airport, or Cellcity in the V&A Waterfront, or arrange this with your car hire.

Faxes can be sent from hotels and many newsagents.

E-mail is well-established. With many hotels, shops, and tourist offices having e-mail addresses, it is an economical and efficient way to research and arrange your trip in advance (see also WEB SITES).

TICKETS

Tickets for concerts, theater, opera and ballet performances, and cinemas are bookable through Computicket. You can call them at Tel. (021) 430 8000 or visit the booth at Victoria Wharf at the V&A Waterfront.

TIME ZONES

Cape Town (and all of South Africa) is two hours ahead of Greenwich Mean Time, seven hours ahead of US Eastern Standard Time year-round and one hour in advance of central European winter time.

TIPPING

Waiters and waitresses should receive 10–15% of the bill, unless a service charge is included already. Taxi drivers, bar tenders, hairdressers and tour guides also expect to receive 10% of the bill. R1–R2 per bag is appropriate for hotel porters, and R20 per week for hotel maids. In addition, all gas stations use attendants, who should be tipped R2–R3 for cleaning your windows and checking oil and water.

TOILETS

Good public toilets can usually be found in shopping centers, gas stations, and tourist attractions. Facilities at National Parks and beaches may be more basic, but the standard of hygiene is usually high. A small charge is sometimes levied.

TOURIST INFORMATION (see also WEB SITES)

Before your trip, contact the South African Tourist Board (SATOUR) branch in your home country. An excellent network of tourist information offices operate throughout the Western Cape. Every region, however small, has its own tourist board, but remember that many of them are not open on Saturdays.

Australia/NZ: 6/285 Clarence Street, Sydney, NSW 2000; Tel (02) 9261 3424.

Canada: Suite 2, 4117 Lawrence Avenue East, Scarborough, Ontario M1E 2S2; Tel/fax (416) 283 0563.

US: 500 Fifth Ave, Suite 2040, New York, NY 10110; Tel (212) 730 2929.

UK: 5-6 Alt Grove, Wimbledon SW19 4DZ; Tel (0208) 944 8080.

When in Cape Town, the following should prove helpful:

Cape Town Tourism and Internet Café, The Pinnacle, corner Burg and Castle streets, Cape Town; Tel. (021) 426 4260; fax (021) 426 4266;e-mail <info@cape-town.org>.

Western Cape Tourism Board; Tel. (021) 914 4613; e-mail <wctb-cape@iafrica.com>.

Winelands Regional Tourism Office; Tel. (021) 872 0686; <e-mail wsto@cis.co.za>.

Garden Route Tourism Marketing; Tel. (044) 874 4040.

W

WEB SITES

Cape Town is definitely turned on to the Internet. It is possible to gather a vast amount of information before you travel, from researching and booking accommodation to helping you decide which museums, restaurants, and attractions are of most interest.

Some useful and informative web sites are:

<www.cape-town.org> (The web site of Cape Town Tourism. The official Visitors Center in the city center is also an Internet café. See also TOURIST INFORMATION.)

<www.mg.co.za> (The web site of the national newspaper, *the Daily Mail & Guardian*. It contains hundreds of links to other web sites of interest, with categories including arts, travel, news, and sports. An outstanding source of online information.)

<www.wcapetourism.co.za> (Western Cape Tourism)

<www.gardenroute.org.za> (Garden Route Tourism)

<www.placestostay.com> (worldwide online accommodation information and booking service)

<www. africa.com> (Covers all African countries. Cape Town-relevant links include individual hotels and attractions, tour operators, online-accommodation services.)

<www.museums.org.za> (links to many of the museums in the city)

<www.waterfront.co.za> (V&A Waterfront, links to many of the shops and attractions)

It is also possible to contact most of the tourist boards by e-mail (see TOURIST INFORMATION)

WEIGHTS AND MEASURES
Distances are shown in kilometers, smaller measurements in centimeters and meters, weight in grams and kilograms, volume in liters and temperatures in degrees Celsius (Centigrade).

Length

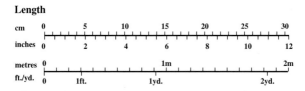

Cape Town

Weight

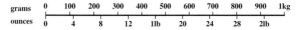

Temperature

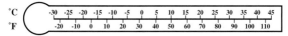

YOUTH HOSTELS

Youth hostels and backpackers' lodges in and around Cape Town are increasing in number all the time. Although accommodation is fairly basic, they usually have cafés and communal kitchens, and many also now offer e-mail and Internet facilities.

A more upmarket type of backpackers' lodge has also recently started to emerge, offering more comfortable, peaceful accommodation than that traditionally found in youth hostels and lodges, but still at very low cost (around $15 per person per night).

There are a host of web sites giving links to youth hostels and lodges, including <www.hostels.com/za.html>. Hostelling International South Africa (web site <www.hisa.org.za>; Tel 021/419 1853) will arrange accommodation in advance in a number of lodges and hostels.

Some of the most comfortable include:

Ashanti Lodge, 11 Hof Street Gardens; Tel (021) 423 8721; e-mail <ashanti@iafrica.com>

The Backpack, 74 New Church Street, Tamboerskloof; Tel (021) 423 4530; e-mail <backpack@gem.co.za>

Cloudbreak, 219 Buitenkant Street; Tel/fax (021) 461 6892; e-mail <cloudbrk@gem.co.za>

Recommended Hotels

The largely undeserved, bad publicity about crime in Cape
Town over the last few years has resulted in an increasing
trend for visitors to choose to stay in the Winelands (30
minutes' drive) or Hermanus (one hour drive). As a result,
hotel rates in and around the city are extremely competitive
and relatively cheap for a major city. To fully enjoy Cape
Town and its many attractions, a stay of at least 3 to 4
nights is recommended.

The hotels below are price-graded and all take major
credit cards. These prices are based on the average cost
of a double room:

$$$$$	over R1000
$$$$	R600 to R1000
$$$	R300 to R600
$$	R150 to R300
$	under R150

IN CAPE TOWN

Breakwater Lodge $$ *Portswood, V&A Waterfront 8002;
Tel. (021) 406 1911; fax (021) 406 1070; e-mail <brkwater@
fortesking-hotels.co.za>*. Former prison now a budget hotel in
superb location. The rooms are basic but comfortable.
Conference facilities. Disabled access. 327 rooms.

The Cape Grace $$$$$ *West Quay, V&A Waterfront, Cape
Town 8002; Tel. (021) 410 7100; fax (021) 419 7622; e-mail
<reservations@capegrace.com>*. Its prime location on the
Waterfront, with wonderful views of Table Mountain, make this

a much sought-after hotel at the luxury end of the market. Family-owned and a member of the Small Luxury Hotels of the World. Swimming pool, private library, boardroom. Disabled access. 102 rooms.

Cape Heritage Hotel $$$$ *90 Bree Street, Cape Town; Tel. (021) 424 4646; fax (021) 424 4949; e-mail <chrelais@satis. co.za>.* Modern facilities in an 18th-century house in the heart of the city, close to Heritage Square and the Bo-Kaap. Ideal for exploring the city and for access to shops and restaurants. Member of Relais Hotels South Africa. Gymnasium. 15 rooms.

Cape Sun International $$$$ *Strand Street, Cape Town 8000; Tel. (021) 488 5100; fax (021) 423 8875; e-mail <capesun@interconti.com>.* Skyscraper hotel situated on the edge of the city center with view of Table Mountain and the V&A Waterfront. Member of Inter-Continental Hotel group. Sauna, fitness center. 388 rooms.

iKhaya Guest Lodge $$$ *Dunkley Square, Gardens, Cape Town; Tel. (021) 461 8880; fax (021) 461 8889.* Splendid wood and stone carvings and sandstone walls emphasize the African ambiance of this comfortable small lodge in the heart of the historic city center. 16 rooms, including some self-catering apartments.

Leeuwenvoet House $$$ *93 New Church Street, Tamboerskloof, Cape Town 8001; Tel. (021) 424 1133; fax (021) 424 0495; e-mail <stay@leeuwenvoet.co.za>.* This historic building is now an enchanting guest house. Charming furnished rooms, good food, and a warm welcome make guests feel that they are friends staying in a Cape Town home rather than guests in a hotel. Swimming pool/hot tub. 11 rooms.

The Mount Nelson $$$$$ *76 Orange Street, Cape Town 8000; Tel. (021) 483 1000; fax (021) 424 7472; e-mail <nellress@iafrica.com>.* This gracious landmark, known affectionately as "the Nellie," is the symbol of elegance and the height of luxury, nestling in the shadow of Table Mountain. From the moment you drive up the palm-fringed avenue to the main entrance you cannot fail to enjoy your stay. Afternoon tea on the terrace is a real treat. An Orient Express hotel and member of the Leading Hotels of the World. Gymnasium, swimming pool, tennis, hair and beauty salon. Disabled access. 226 rooms.

The Victoria & Alfred $$$$ *V&A Waterfront, Cape Town 8002; Tel. (021) 419 6677; fax (021) 419 8955; e-mail <res@v-and-a.co.za>.* All rooms have views of Table Mountain or Table Bay, and its location means that all the shops, restaurants, and leisure activities of the Waterfront are on the doorstep. Modern conference facilities. Disabled access. 68 rooms.

Villa Via $$$$ *Beach Road, Granger Bay, Waterfront 8002; Tel. (021) 418 5729; fax (021) 418 5717; e-mail <vvgv@iafrica.com>.* Waterfront location with private marina make Cape Town's newest luxury hotel a convenient top-of-the-market choice. All rooms enjoy good views. Swimming pool, beauty salon, and spa. 182 rooms.

OUTSIDE THE CITY CENTER

The Bay Hotel $$$$$ *Victoria Road, Camps Bay 8040; Tel. (021) 438 4444; fax (021) 438 4455; e-mail <res@thebay.co.za>.*

All rooms enjoy views of the Atlantic Ocean or the Twelve Apostles and Table Mountain. The hotel overlooks the beach of this trendy resort just 10 minutes from central Cape Town. Member of the Small Luxury Hotels of the World. Swimming pool. 77 rooms.

The Cellars Hohenort $$$$$ *93 Brommersvlei Road, Constantia 7800; Tel. (021) 794 2137; fax (021) 794 2149; e-mail <cellars@ct.lia.net>.* Sister hotel to The Plettenberg (Plettenberg Bay) and The Marine Hotel (Hermanus), this delightful hotel in beautiful landscaped gardens is a taste of luxury in the Southern Suburbs. Two swimming pools, tennis court. 56 rooms.

Colona Castle $$$ *1 Verwoerd Street, off Boyes Drive, Muizenberg 7943; Tel. (021) 788 8235; fax (021) 788 6577; e-mail <colona@link.co.za>.* Small, privately-owned guest house on the mountainside above Muizenberg with a great panoramic view. Friendly with excellent service. Swimming pool. Six rooms.

Steenberg Country Hotel $$$$$ *Steenberg Estate, Constantia Valley 7945; Tel. (021) 713 2222; fax (021) 713 2221; e-mail <hotel@iafrica.com>.* This wine estate dates back to 1682, with rooms in the old Cape Dutch Manor House, the Jonkerhuis, and the restored barn; some, furnished with antiques. Swimming pool, golf, winery. 19 rooms.

Vineyard Hotel $$$$ *Colinton Road, Newlands 7700; Tel (021) 683 3044; fax (021) 683 3365.* Experience outstanding Colonial elegance in "Paradise", the Cape Dutch house, now a national monument, built in 1799 for socialite Lady Anne

Barnard. The fine gardens boast superb views. Swimming pool. Two restaurants, including the award-winning Au Jardin. Disabled access. 160 rooms.

WEST COAST

Bushmanskloof Wilderness Reserve $$$$ *R344, Kenilworth; Tel. (021) 797 0990; fax (021) 761 5551; e-mail <santrack@ilink.nis.za>*. This thatched lodge in the Cederberg Mountains offers the chance to experience the beauty of the region, to view its wildlife such as Cape Mountain zebra and gemsbok in their natural habitat and to see some fine examples of Bushman rock art. In spring the valley is carpeted in colorful wildflowers. Member of Relais & Chateaux. Swimming pool. Ten rooms.

The Farmhouse Guesthouse $$$ *5 Egret Street, Langebaan 7357; Tel (02287) 22062; fax (02287) 21980*. Comfortable accommodation in a mid-19th century farmhouse close to the West Coast National Marine Park, with views of the stunning Langebaan Lagoon. Swimming pool. 15 rooms.

Overberg

Arniston Hotel $$$ *Arniston Hotel, Arniston; Tel. (028) 475 9000; fax (021) 475 9633*. A modern-looking hotel located on the seafront of the beautiful Arniston Bay, a short walk from the harbor and fisherman's cottages. Some rooms with superb view. Friendly, helpful staff make your stay a delight. Disabled access. 30 rooms.

Auberge Burgundy $$$$$ *16 Harbour Road, Hermanus 7200; Tel. (028) 313 1201; fax (028) 313 1204; e-mail <auberge@hermanus.co.za>*. Luxury Provençale-style guest house in the center of town. Beautiful courtyards and gardens. Swimming pool. 18 rooms.

The Marine Hotel $$$$$ *Marine Drive, Hermanus 7200; Tel. (028) 370 1000; fax (028) 370 0160; e-mail <marine@ hermanus.co.za>.* Sister hotel to The Plettenberg (Plettenberg Bay) and The Cellars Hohenort (Constantia), this luxury hotel on the clifftop is perfect for whale-watching. Swimming pool. 47 rooms.

Whale Rock Lodge $$$ *26 Springfield Avenue, Hermanus 7200; Tel (0283) 700014; fax (0283) 22932.* Attractive, small thatched lodge, just a short walk from one of the best whale-watching locations in the area. Swimming pool. 11 rooms.

Stellenbosch Wine Route

L'Auberge du Quartier Francais $$$$ *16/18 Huguenot Street, Franschhoek; Tel. (021) 876 2151; fax (021) 876 3105; e-mail <res@lqf.co.za>.* A hidden gem, set in beautiful and fragrant gardens, adjacent to Franschhoek's most famous restaurant Le Quartier Français (see page 142). Swimming pool, complimentary mini-bar. 17 rooms.

Die Ou Pasterie $$ *41 Lourens Street, Somerset West 7130; Tel. (021) 852 2120; fax (021) 851 3710; e-mail <pastorie@ iafrica.com>.* A charming guesthouse adjoining one of the Cape's best restaurants (also called Die Ou Pasterie, see page 142), in a relaxing location with good views. Swimming pool, Victorian pub. 16 rooms.

D'Ouwe Werf $$$ *30 Church Street, Stellenbosch 7600; Tel. (021) 887 4608; fax (021) 887 4626; e-mail <ouwewerf@*

iafrica.com>. Friendly, helpful staff and good food at this delightfully historic inn in the heart of old Stellenbosch. Shady courtyard for relaxing breakfasts, lunches, or teas. Swimming pool. 25 rooms.

Grand Roche $$$$$ *Plantasie Street, Paarl 7622; Tel. (021) 863 2727; fax (021) 863 2220; e-mail <reserve@granderoche. co.za>*. Renowned for its famous Bosman's restaurant, this luxury hotel is set amongst the vineyards of Paarl. Amenitites include gymnasium, two swimming pools, tennis, massage, sauna, steam-room. 35 rooms.

Lanzerac Manor & Winery $$$$ *Lanzerac Road, Stellenbosch 7600; Tel. (021) 887 1132; fax (021) 887 2310; e-mail <info@lanzerac.co.za>*. One of South Africa's most gracious country hotels set in its own 300-year-old wine estate; a quiet location at the start of the Jonkershoek Valley. Swimming pool, conference facilities. 40 rooms.

The Garden Route

Belvidere Manor $$$$ *Belvidere Estate, Knysna 6570; Tel. (044) 387 1055; fax (044) 387 1059; e-mail <manager@ belvidere.co.za>*. Relaxing location overlooking Knysna Lagoon and the town. Reception and dining and sitting rooms are in the Manor House but guests stay in cottages, with verandas and fireplaces, in 10 acres of gardens. Swimming pool. 30 cottages.

Fancourt Hotel & Country Club Estate $$$$$ *Montagu Street, Blanco, George 6530; Tel. (044) 870 8282; fax (044) 870 7605; e-mail <hotel@fancourt.co.za>*. A golf-lover's paradise on one of South Africa's finest courses. The old Manor House at the heart of the hotel is a national monument. Amenitites include swimming pools, tennis, bowls, squash, golf. 100 rooms.

Hog Hollow Country Lodge $$$ *Askop Road, Plettenberg Bay 6600; Tel. (044) 534 8879; fax (044) 534 8879; e-mail <hoghollow@global.co.za>.* Hotel in a private nature reserve, 15 minutes drive from Plettenberg Bay. Swimming pool. 12 rooms.

Hoogekraal $$$ *P.O.Box 34, George 6530; Tel. (044) 879 1277; fax (044) 879 1300; e-mail <guests@ hoogekraal. co.za>.* This former homestead of the Botha family is now a country house hotel where guests stay in the farmhouse rooms, furnished with antiques of the period when each building was erected. Candlelit dinners in the antique-furnished dining room, hosted by the owner, Tim Botha, nephew of the former South African Premier, are both entertaining and memorable. Seven rooms.

Hunter's Country House $$$$$ *Pear Tree Farm, Plettenberg Bay 6600; Tel. (044) 532 7818; fax (043) 532 7878; e-mail <hunters@pixie.co.za>.* Luxury country house hotel which offers warm, personalized service of the highest quality. Swimming pool. Member of Relais & Chateaux. 23 garden suites.

Little Karoo

Rosenhof Country Lodge $$ *264 Baron Van Rheede Street, Oudtshoorn 6620; Tel. (044) 272 2232; fax (044) 272 3021.* Delightful hotel with rooms opening onto a rose garden. Good food served in dining room of main house. 12 rooms.

Recommended Restaurants

Eating out in the Western Cape is a great pleasure, and one that can be enjoyed even on a budget. Dining in South Africa is relatively cheap by European standards and good value even for Americans. The standard of food is generally good and the cosmopolitan nature of Cape Town means that visitors are spoiled for choice. Below are a selection of restaurants which offer good food, service, and, in many cases, a delightful setting. There are lots more so don't be afraid to look beyond these listings.

In general, staff in cafés and restaurants earn a pittance and are therefore dependent on tips to take home a good wage. As a result, the standard of service tends to be good. A tip of 10 to 15% of the cost of the meal is the accepted norm.

The restaurants below are price-graded. These prices are based on the average cost of a three-course meal, excluding wine and tips:

$$$$$	over R150
$$$$	R100 to R150
$$$	R75 to R100
$$	R50 to R75
$	under R50

IN CAPE TOWN

Aubergine $$$$ *39 Barnet Street, Gardens; Tel. (021) 465 4909.* Lunch on weekdays; dinner daily; Sunday dinner only during summer season. Exquisite classical French/Continental cuisine with good selection of vegetarian dishes. Cape and imported wines. Corkage R20. Major credit cards.

...and Lemon $$$ *98 Shortmarket Street, city center; Tel. (021) 423 4873.* Lunch and dinner Monday–Saturday. Bright and fashionable restaurant with good food from around the world. Vegetarian options. Small wine list of in-vogue wines. Corkage R20. Major credit cards.

Bukhara $$$ *33 Church Street, city center; Tel. (021) 424 0000.* Lunch Monday–Saturday; dinner daily. Busy gourmet Indian restaurant with fine food. Vegetarian options. Corkage R20. Major credit cards.

Bonthuys $$$$ *121 Castle Street, city center; Tel (021) 426 2368.* Dinner only Tuesday–Saturday. Restaurant with a difference; bizarre décor and crockery deliberately mismatched. Food combinations are equally unusual, but delicious. Limited wine list so bring your own. No corkage fee. Major credit cards.

Café Bardeli $$ *Longkloof Studios, Darter Street (off Kloof Street), Gardens; Tel. (021) 423 4444.* Breakfast, lunch, teas and dinner daily. Great place to hang out and relax. Major credit cards.

Cape Colony $$$$$ *Mount Nelson Hotel, city center; Tel. (021) 483 1000.* Breakfast, lunch, and dinner daily. Wonderful South African food, including Cape Malay dishes, in the grandest old hotel in Cape Town. Vegetarian options. Wines for all tastes. Corkage R20. Major credit cards.

Cape Manna $$$ *34 Napier Street, De Waterkant; Tel (021) 419 2181.* Dinner Tuesday–Saturday. This tiny restaurant, with red walls and star-studded blue ceiling, serves Cape food at its best. Vegetarian options. Unlicensed — bring your own wine. No corkage fee. Major credit cards.

De Goewerneur $$ *Castle of Good Hope, Darling Street, city center; Tel. (021) 461 4895.* Lunch and dinner Monday–Saturday. Colonial restaurant serving Cape Malay and international food and snacks inside the Castle. Limited wine list. Major credit cards.

The Green Dolphin Jazz Restaurant $$$ *Victoria and Alfred Mall, Pierhead, V&A Waterfront; Tel (021) 421 7471.* Hear some of the best Cape Town jazz around playing every night at this sophisticated bistro which specializes in ostrich meat and seafood. Major credit cards.

The Happy Wok $$$ *62A Kloof Street, Gardens; Tel. (021) 424 2423/2455.* Lunch Monday–Friday; dinner daily. Delicious cuisine from all over Asia. Vegetarian options. Major credit cards.

Hildebrand $$ *Pierhead, V&A Waterfront; Tel. (021) 425 3385.* Lunch and dinner daily. Classic Italian *trattoria* on the Waterfront. Vegetarian options. Comprehensive wine list plus good selection of cocktails and aperitifs. Corkage R12.50. Major credit cards.

Miller's Thumb $$$ *10B Kloofnek Road, Tamboerskloof; Tel. (021) 424 3838.* Lunch Tuesday–Friday; dinner Monday to Saturday. Seafood with an international flavor, in lively surroundings. Small wine list. Corkage R10. Major credit cards.

Noon Gun Tearoom and Restaurant $ *273 Longmarket Street, Signal Hill, Cape Town 8001; Tel. (021) 424 0529.* Lunch, teas, and dinner Monday–Saturday. Tea-room and restaurant which serves Cape Malay food, including *halaal* dishes, at the foot of Signal Hill. Vegetarian options. No alcohol served or permitted. Major credit cards.

Ocean Basket $$ *75 Kloof Street, Gardens; Tel. (021) 422 0322.* Lunch Monday–Saturday. Part of a restaurant chain, this is a great place to eat seafood. Busy and fun. Limited wine list. Major credit cards.

Quay West $$$$ *Cape Grace Hotel, V&A Waterfront; Tel. (021) 418 0520.* Breakfast, lunch, teas, and dinner daily. Fine restaurant in hotel voted "best small luxury hotel in the world, 1999." Diners enjoy wonderful view of Table Mountain.

Vegetarian options. Excellent and expansive wine list. Corkage R20. Major credit cards.

Rozenhof $$$$ *18 Kloof Street, Gardens; Tel. (021) 424 1968.* Lunch Monday–Friday; dinner Monday–Saturday. Comfortable and informal dining in a historic house with yellowwood ceilings. Good wine list, with many available by the glass. Corkage R12.50. Major credit cards.

Rustica $$ *70 New Church Street, city center; Tel. (021) 423 5474.* Lunch Monday–Friday; dinner daily. Rustic Italian food including pasta and pizza. Good-value wines by the glass. Corkage R8. Major credit cards.

Savoy Cabbage $$$$ *Heritage Square, city center; Tel. (021) 424 2626.* Lunch Monday–Friday; dinner Monday–Saturday. Gracious champagne bar and restaurant with frequently changing menu. Wonderful seafood and many vegetarian dishes. Good selection of well-priced wines. Corkage R20. Major credit cards.

OUTSIDE THE CITY CENTER

Africa Café $$$ *213 Lower Main Road, Observatory; Tel. (021) 447 9553.* Dinner Monday–Saturday; lunch by arrangement. Also at 108 Shortmarket Street, city center. Dishes from all over Africa and some unusual flavors. Vegetarian options. Cape wines and African fruit cocktails. Major credit cards.

Au Jardin $$$$ *Vineyard Hotel, Newlands; Tel (021) 683 1520.* Lunch Tuesday–Friday; dinner Monday to Saturday. French haute cuisine with marvelous views. Cape and imported wines. Bring-your-own-wines discouraged, but corkage R20. Major credit cards.

Black Marlin $$$ *Main Road, Miller's Point, Simon's Town; Tel. (021) 786 3876.* Lunch daily; dinner Monday– Saturday. Famous seafood restaurant in an old whaling station. Excellent food and fine views. Good wine list. Major credit cards.

Blues $$$ *The Promenade, Victoria Road, Camps Bay; Tel. (021) 438 2040.* Lunch and dinner daily. Trendy and fashionable restaurant with appealing menu. Vegetarian options. Major credit cards.

Café Pescado $$$ *118 St. George's Street, Simon's Town; Tel. (021) 786 2272.* Breakfast, lunch, teas and dinner daily. Seafood any way you like it in a casual environment. Ordinary wine list. Enjoy its good selection of beers. Corkage R10. Major credit cards.

Constantia Uitsig $$$$ *Uitsig Farm, Spaanschematriver Road, Constantia; Tel. (021) 794 4480.* Lunch Tuesday– Sunday; dinner daily; booking essential. Contemporary cuisine with a Mediterranean feel. Excellent seafood. Vegetarian options. Wine list includes best from the Cape and Constantia Uitsig's own label. Corkage R15. Major credit cards.

Emily's Bistro $$$$ *77 Roodebloem Road, Woodstock; Tel. (021) 448 2366.* Lunch Tuesday–Friday; dinner Monday– Saturday. Bistro with its own culinary school. Vegetarian options. Fabulous selection of wines to suit every budget. Bring your own, if you must. Corkage R20. Major credit cards.

Fish on the Rocks $ *Far end of Harbour Road, Hout Bay; Tel. (021) 790 1153.* Open 365 days a year but closes at 8pm. Superb local fish, or calamari, and chips in outdoor setting with view across Hout Bay to Chapman's Peak. Unlicensed. Major credit cards accepted but so cheap you won't even need to use them!

Jonkershuis $$$ *Groot Constantia Estate, Constantia; Tel. (021) 794 6255.* A little bit of everything from Cape country in a delightful setting. Only estate wines. Bring-your-own discouraged. Corkage R15. Major credit cards.

Parks $$$ *114 Constantia Road, Constantia; Tel. (021) 797 8202.* Dinner Monday–Saturday. Fine African cuisine in a Victorian cottage. Vegetarian options. Good wine list at reasonable prices, with a list of recommendations. Bring-your-own discouraged. Major credit cards.

EXCURSIONS

West Coast

Die Strandloper $$$ *On the beach, Langebaan; Tel. (022) 772 2490 / 083 227 7195.* Lunch and dinner daily in summer, call for availability at other times of the year. A not-to-be-missed experience. Ten-course meal including every local seafood you can imagine. Eat as much or as little as you like. Swim or sunbathe between courses. Unlicensed. Cash only.

Overberg

Arniston Hotel $$$$ *Arniston Hotel, Arniston; Tel. (028) 475 9000.* Breakfast, lunch, and dinner daily. Restaurant with breathtaking view across the harbor and Arniston Bay offers fine food in a friendly environment. The seafood is especially good. Limited wine list of good wines. Major credit cards.

Bientang's Cave $$$$$ *Beachfront, Hermanus; Tel. (028) 312 3452.* Seafood served in a cave open to the ocean. You can eat inside or out; either way, the location is spectacular. The prices aren't cheap, but few places offer the chance to whale-watch as you enjoy fine food. Opening hours vary, and it is best to call and check. Licensed. Major credit cards.

Breede River Valley and Little Karoo

Paddagang $$$ *23 Church Street, Tulbagh; Tel (023) 630 0242.* Breakfast and lunch daily. Dinner on Saturday only. The name of this relaxed eatery means "frog," and frogs feature on the labels of the locally-produced wine served here. The menu features good traditional regional cooking. The building is a national monument (1821), and the gardens are charming. Major credit cards.

Stellenbosch Wine Route

96 Winery Road $$$$ *Off R44 between Somerset West and Stellenbosch; Tel. (021) 842 2020.* Lunch daily; dinner Monday–Saturday. Excellent country restaurant offering mix of Cape, Eastern, and French influences. Incredible wine list to suit all budgets and walk in cellar. Corkage R10. Major credit cards.

Bosman's $$$$$ *Grande Roche Hotel, Plantasie Street, Paarl; Tel. (021) 863 2727.* Breakfast, lunch, and dinner daily. Africa's only restaurant to achieve Relais Gourmand status offers top-class international cuisine, with special tastings by arrangement. Huge wine list to cater for every taste. Corkage R30. Major credit cards.

Decameron $$ *50 Plein Street, Stellenbosch; Tel. (021) 883 3331.* Lunch and dinner daily. Traditional Italian restaurant with delicious specialties of the house. Wine list of Stellenbosch wines. Corkage R8.50. Major credit cards.

D'Ouwe Werf $$$ *30 Church Street, Stellenbosch; Tel. (021) 886 5671.* Breakfast, lunch, teas, and dinner daily. Fine food to suit all tastes and appetites in this delightfully welcoming historic inn in the heart of old Stellenbosch. Shady courtyard for breakfast for relaxing breakfasts, lunches, or teas. Wine list offers best of Stellenbosch wines. Corkage R6. Major credit cards.

Die Ou Pasterie $$$$ *41 Lourens Street, Somerset West; Tel. (021) 852 2120.* Breakfast daily; lunch Tuesday–Friday, dinner Monday–Saturday. Fine cuisine in an early 19th-century parsonage, with seasonal offerings. Award-winning wine list with suggestions to compliment food. Corkage R10. Major credit cards.

Le Quartier Français $$$ *16/18 Huguenot Street, Franschhoek; Tel. (021) 876 2151.* Breakfast, lunch, teas, and dinner daily. The restaurant which founded Franschhoek's reputation for fine food offers a delightful selection of haute cuisine. Superb wine list with especially good selection of local wines. Major credit cards.

Wijnhuis $$$$ *Andringa Street, Stellenbosch; Tel. (021) 887 5844.* Breakfast, lunch, and dinner daily. Essential for all visitors to Stellenbosch. Restaurant/wine bar/wine shop combination makes for a great introduction to the wines of Stellenbosch. Wine tasting menu changes daily and permits tasting of six wines for R17. Stocks wines from over 40 Stellenbosch estates to buy or drink with the excellent food. Often busy. Corkage R10. Major credit cards.

The Garden Route

The Copper Pot $$$ *12 Montagu Street, Blanco, George; Tel. (044) 870 7378.* Lunch Monday–Friday; dinner daily. Elegant old house serving French and South African dishes. Excellent wine list to suit all budgets. Corkage R10. Major credit cards.

Phantom Forest Lodge $$$$ *Phantom Pass, near Knysna; Tel. (044) 387 1923.* Breakfast, lunch, and dinner daily. One to be experienced. Hilltop wonderland of bamboo and thatch with treetop plank walkways between buildings. Regularly changing set menu of cuisine from across Africa. Good wine list of South African wines. Major credit cards.

INDEX